THE STARK GUIDE TO ORIENTAL RUGS AND CARPETS

GRACIE MANSION, NEW YORK CITY MAYOR'S RESIDENCE
Room designed by Mark Hampton

THE STARK GUIDE TO ORIENTAL RUGS AND CARPETS

with an Introduction by Jon Thompson

Text type was set in Goudy
Designed by Sullivan Scully Design Group
Edited by Nicky Leach

Copyright ©1996 by John Stark
All rights reserved.

This book may not be reproduced in whole or in part, by any means
(with the exception of short quotes for the purpose of review),
without permission of the publisher.

ISBN 0-9651501-0-0

Printed in Hong Kong by Dai Nippon Printing Co. Ltd.

Cover and back cover: Plate 71

Stark® CARPET

EXECUTIVE OFFICE
AND MAIN SHOWROOM
D&D BUILDING
979 THIRD AVENUE
NEW YORK, NY 10022

Telephone: 212•752•9000
Fax: 212•758•4342

PACIFIC DESIGN CENTER
8687 MELROSE AVENUE
LOS ANGELES, CA 90069
Telephone: 213•657•8275

SHOWROOMS: ATLANTA/BOSTON
CHARLOTTE/CHICAGO/CLEVELAND
DALLAS/DANIA/DENVER
HOUSTON/LONDON/LOS ANGELES
PHILADELPHIA/PHOENIX/PITTSBURGH
RALEIGH/SAN FRANCISCO
SCOTTSDALE/SEATTLE/TROY
WASHINGTON D.C.

The Library at Wimpole Hall
Picture Courtesy of The National Trust

Preface

Our objective in publishing this book has been to display a selection of beautiful antique carpets that many of our interior designer friends have used to enhance the magnificent beauty of a room. We have included an historical introduction, by Dr. Jon Thompson. This introduction describes the art of carpet weaving, as well as the culture and lifestlye of the artists who weave them. In his article, written exclusively for this book, Mr. Thompson also comments on some of the plates in *The Collections*.

In *The Collections*, the authors have given their poetic impressions of each carpet's unique beauty and characteristics, rather than explaining specific histories and techniques.

It is interesting to note that very little has changed as far as the public's taste for carpets is concerned. Nearly all of the carpets in this collection were originally commissioned by Europeans or Americans in the late 19th century. Although the carpets may have been woven in Persia, India or Turkey, nearly all of them were made for homes in Europe and America. That is why almost no decorative carpets remain in the countries that wove them, although they are available at various auction houses and dealers in Europe and America.

John Stark

Room designed by Thomas Allardyce and Illya Hendrix, Hendrix and Allardyce, Los Angeles
photograph by Mary E. Nichols

We would like to acknowledge the following people for their support in making this project possible:

———⋄———

Dr. Jon Thompson, *Introduction Author*

Julie Sullivan, *Book Design*

Ziba Bolour, *Production Manager*

Jack Haldane, *Author*

James Hawkins, *Author*

Anthony Thompson, *Captions*

Peter Williams, *Photographer*

Hussein Montazaran, *Photographer*

Alfonso Serrano, *Printing Coordinator*

THE EASTERN CARPET *and the* WEST

by JON THOMPSON

A nomadic family of the Qashqa'i tribe at home in their tent. The Qashqa'i who live in the central Zagros mountains of Persia, are excellent weavers, and the colorful covers draped over the storage pile at the back of the tent were made by these women from the wool of their own sheep. The boy is sitting on a felt, the normal, every day floor-covering in the tent. Not every family owns piled carpets, and only the wealthy keep them on the floor all the time.

FROM MY EARLIEST YEARS I have memories of carpets on the floors at home. Their patterns were a source of endless fascination. I would look again and again at the way they linked up with one another, how the same motif appeared in various places in the rug in different colors, and how designs that at first sight seemed to be the same were subject to countless little variations. In one rug, there was a branching design in a narrow border that wound its way all round the edge of the rug but did not quite meet up in one corner, just like the inner border of the Bijar rug (see page 15). In another, there was a change in the main background color part of the way along it, as in the Tabriz (see page 18) only much more noticeable. I wondered in my childish mind if two people might have worked on it, one beginning at each end until they met in the middle—something I now know to be impossible.

Later in my life, the processes of carpet-making became a subject of absorbing interest for me and I began to understand how and why the things that had fascinated me as a child had come to be the way they were. Far from removing the mystery and magic of those friends of my childhood, my researches and studies have actually increased my appreciation of their subtle art and the skill of their makers.

Knowing what I do now, it strikes me that those who care enough to want handmade carpets as companions in their home might also be interested to know something about the remarkable series of labor-intensive processes involved in their production—the more so because the amount of time it takes to make a carpet is almost unthinkable in an age that measures the cost of labor by the minute.

For some reason, there is a prevailing misconception about how hand-knotted carpets are made. It seems to me that this false idea derives from the fashion for what are called 'hooked rugs,' produced by poking little tufts of wool or strips of cotton fabric through a prepared, loosely woven canvas using a metal tool specially made for the purpose. Many people have told me that they remember older relatives working on such rugs, and it was even fashionable at one time to give children 'carpet-making' kits as a present. This technique, however has nothing whatever to do with the traditional craft of carpet weaving and is, strictly speaking, a form of embroidery.

It was not long ago that people made many of the textiles they needed at home. Even today, there are nomads in Iran and Turkey who weave an extraordinary variety of functional items: long strips of goat hair cloth for

The Eastern Carpet and the West

the roof of their tents, blankets, covers, sacks, storage bags, pouches, saddle bags, and even woolen material for clothing. Nomads also weave rugs and carpets, and they have been making them for centuries, perhaps millennia. All these things were made for their own use and were rarely traded—when something was worn out it was thrown away and a new one made. As a result, nomadic weavings were hardly known outside the circle of their own society.

The tent floor was routinely covered with felt, a cheaper fabric made without the use of a loom. The cost

of making a carpet, including the materials and dyestuffs, was such that only the wealthier nomads could afford to have knotted pile carpets on the floor of their tents for every- day use. Most nomadic families would own one or more floor rug but these would be reserved for the use of guests or brought out only on special occasions.

In the 1860s and 1870s, two things happened at the same time to make nomadic weavings better known in the West. The first was an awakening of interest in Europe and America in what came to be known as the "Oriental" carpet. (For many people the "Orient" extends much farther east than the principal carpet-weaving regions that concern us—Turkey, Persia, the Caucasus Turkestan and India. In spite of that, the term "Oriental carpet" seems to be with us for good.) The second was a profound change in the social and political climate of carpet-producing countries in the Near East, which made it difficult for nomads to continue their traditional way of life. Many nomadic families were forced to settle and become farmers or move to the cities to look for work. When they ceased to be nomads they no longer had need of all the bags, pouches, rugs, and other textiles associated with the mobile life so they sold them. Anything remotely saleable was shipped to the West to cater for the new demand for "Oriental" rugs of every kind. In this way many nomadic weavings found their way into Western homes. Few people, including the dealers, had any idea where they had come from, what they were, or who had made them.

Two Qashqa'i weavers begin work on a piled carpet. They weave on a horizontal loom, working from memory without any cartoon or instruction. The beams are held in place by stout wooden pegs driven into the ground.

Above
Nomads of the Karakoyunlu tribe in the central Taurus mountains of Turkey get ready for their autumn migration southwards to low-lying land near the Mediterranean coast. The black, goat-hair tent cloth is ready packed in two large loads. Other bundles are wrapped in a home-made flat-woven blanket and kilim. The last thing to be dismantled and packed is the loom because a large bag needed for the journey is not yet finished.

PLATE 8, SULTANABAD
The squarish shape, non-traditional colors and innovative design of this piece are typical of the carpets produced in the late nineteenth century by the merchant entrepreneurs of Sultanabad. Foreseeing a great revival of carpet weaving in Persia driven by demand from the West, it was they who took steps to produce the specific shapes, colors and sizes required for this rapidly expanding market.

One of the main difficulties of the nomadic way of life is that everything a nomad owns must be portable. Their looms cannot be very large because the beams would be too heavy to transport. Thus most of the things they made were of modest size. In western homes these items, in effect the nomads' furniture, were put to new use as scatter rugs, cushions, magazine holders, and even upholstery material. Though these smaller weavings were extremely popular, and remain so today, what people in the prosperous West really wanted was larger to furnish their living rooms. The largest nomadic carpets were something around 7 feet wide with a length to match, of 10 feet—hardly a room-size.

In Persian towns and villages it was the custom, and indeed still is today, to have no furniture in the way of tables or chairs in the main living room. People sit on the floor, often leaning against a cushion. For eating, a special cloth is put on the floor and the food is laid out on it. Likewise, with the addition of pillows and blankets, the floor serves for sleeping. During the day the bedding is piled up at one end of the room in a neat stack.

Village-looms tend to be larger that those used by the nomads, but here too there are limits. To buy a large loom plus all the materials needed to make a large carpet would require a capital investment beyond the means of the average household. The way they got round this problem was to furnish the main room in their home with four carpets. At the sides of the room where people sat were two long narrow rugs (*kénareh*), sold today in the West as 'runners.' At the 'head' of the room across one end was a somewhat wider rug (*kaleh*), and in the center a much larger 'middle carpet', usually about $9^1/2$ feet by about 14. A typical example of the 'middle carpet,' which is shown on page 15, was woven in the village of Bijar, source of some of the sturdiest and most attractive of all Persian village rugs. The designs of all four carpets formed a matching ensemble. At a later date, when quite large looms became more common, someone had the idea of making the four-carpet set as a single carpet on a wide loom. These curious carpets would have been made for the local market and are occasionally found in the West, where they are called, for want of a better term, 'triclinium carpets.' (The triclinium was a dining room in ancient Greece with three couches, used also by the Romans.)

The Eastern Carpet and the West

THE RISING DEMAND in the West for carpets had a major impact on the village weavers. Merchants kept coming round the villages asking for both old and new rugs. The stock of old rugs held in homes was soon exhausted and in the last quarter of the nineteenth century market demand was such that weaving at all levels throughout the Caucasus, Turkey and Persia entered a period of rapid and unprecedented growth.

It soon became evident that the four carpet arrangement which had long satisfied Persian householders was not suitable for American homes. What people wanted was reasonably priced, larger, more square carpets to cover most of the floor. This called for a major change in the way things were done. The first to understand the need for change were the merchants, who quickly set up commercial operations specifically to produce the sizes and patterns required for the western market. They introduced wider looms, financed the dyeing of wool and distributed the necessary yarns to the weavers. A major center for such production sprang up in Sultanabad, (now called Arak) in the late 1870s. An example of the 'new' Sultanabad production made at that time is shown on page 12, opposite. A rug of this rather square shape would never have been found in a traditional Persian home. It is, however, typical of the shapes and sizes made for the burgeoning American market.

The merchants of Sultanabad (and elsewhere) not only organized the production of carpets in the new sizes wanted in America, but they also experimented with patterns and color combinations that might be more popular with western customers than the traditional designs made for the Persian market. Here the merchants were faced with the problem of how to transmit to the weavers the new patterns they wanted to be produced.

The need for patterns suitable for the new market brings us to the question of how carpet patterns are produced in general. I mentioned the popular misconception that oriental carpets are produced in the same way as hooked rugs. The importance of understanding how carpets are actually made lies in the distinction between a fabric built up by working on any part of it—embroidery and hooked rugs—and one built up by weaving, that is adding

In the villages, a hand-powered spinning wheel replaces the simple drop spindle used by nomads. Five or more separate yarns, each prepared in a special way, and of different weight and twist, are used for the various parts of a carpet: the warp, weft, pile, side finish etc. Karagömlek, western Turkey.

The village dyer at work dyeing wool with indigo in the village of Süleyman Köy, western Turkey. Indigo is dissolved in the vat by a process of reduction. In solution, it is almost colorless, but on exposure to air the wool becomes blue-green, changing rapidly to blue. In former times, nomads and villagers would gather dye plants and do their own dyeing to produce the various shades of red, purple, rose, yellow, orange, and black they needed. The blues and greens were more difficult since they involved the use of indigo. Before the invention of chemical reducing agents, dyeing with indigo was a specialized, village-based craft that required large dye-pots, plenty of time, and much practical skill. Today, indigo dyeing is so easy that it can be done at home.

PLATE 11, BAKHSHAYISH
The many irregularities in the design of this charming carpet indicate that it was not woven from a cartoon. It is probably copied from another carpet which was itself a copy. The ultimate origin of the pattern was most likely a costly silk. Fine textiles have been the source of many village rug designs throughout the centuries.

Looms in the villages tend to be larger than those used by nomads and have more technical refinements. This family is making quite a small rug, although the loom is big enough for a fair-sized carpet. Örençik, western Turkey.

horizontal or transverse threads one at a time to a prepared and fixed set of longitudinal threads, which applies to all woven structures, including carpets.

A carpet is built up line by line beginning at one end and working slowly through to the other. What is done cannot be altered afterward. This means that a carpet pattern must be exactly planned in advance. Some simple patterns can be memorized. This method of pattern formation is typically found in nomadic and in some traditional village weavings. Memory-based patterns tend to be rather small in scale, devoid of complex curved lines, and are often arranged in an endless repeat. It is inconceivable that the large, complex and accurately curved field design of the Tabriz carpet, shown on page 18, could have been memorized.

The most common method of pattern formation in villages in former times was, and to a degree still is today, copying. The weavers take a rug and work from the back where the pattern is easier to read. They then copy it as best they can, knot for knot, line by line. Some weavers, such as the Qashqa'i of southern Persia are very good at this, though more often the work of the copyist can only be described as approximate. The problems associated with copying become clear when we try to imagine what happens when the copy itself becomes the model for the next copy. All the mistakes, inaccuracies, simplifications, and omissions are repeated and new ones added. By degrees, the copied pattern takes on a life of its own, departing farther and farther from the original. An example of the end product of this process is the Bakhshayish, shown left, which has a rather large-scale pattern, executed in a distinctly rustic and somewhat approximate way, consisting of a tree flanked by two birds facing each other. This pattern repeats in the width of the rug, and about two-thirds of the way along it is turned upside down. This device of repeating in the width then turning upside down is a typical trick used by the weavers of complex textiles, such as costly silks. They do this to create a good effect using a single unit of pattern in a variety of ways. The carpet weaver has no need of such a device, especially as this carpet was woven without an accurate pattern guide. We can, therefore, be sure that the original of this carpet pattern was copied from an expensive textile and that the copies were in turn copied until we finish up with this rather charmingly naive result.

An even better illustration of the effect of copying is provided by a comparison between the Tabriz carpet, page 16, and the Bijar, page 15. The field design of the Tabriz consists of an apparently complicated arrangement of split leaves. A careful look reveals that they are all joined together rather like the tracery of a wrought iron gate, and that the gaps in the tracery are filled with flowers. This tracery of split-leaves is a traditional Islamic design, known as Arabesque, and dates back to the sixteenth century and beyond. It has been used and re-used countless times throughout the centuries and remains as popular today as it ever was. Here it is accurately worked (by a process we shall discuss later) in sweeping curves that attract the eye and invite one to explore its detail.

The Bijar has a design built on the same principles. (The relationship is more obvious if the carpet is turned at right angles). It too has the split leaf grille with flowers filling the gaps. It is not exactly the same design but belongs to the same "family." The most noticeable difference is that, compared to the Tabriz, the curves in the design of the Bijar are more hesitant: they tend to become a series of straight lines and angles and the form of the split-leaves in the Bijar is distinctly clumsy. Likewise, the flowers are rather abbreviated: in places there are clusters of florets with no stem linking them together. These features in the Bijar reveal the typical results of copying.

It should be stressed here that no value judgement is intended in comparing these two carpets. The Bijar is what one might call a 'vintage thoroughbred.' The weavers of Bijar, some of the most conservative in the country, stuck tenaciously to their traditional vegetable dyes when a lot of new, easy-to-use chemical dyes were available in the cities. They never changed their time-consuming weaving technique, which guaranteed an almost indestructible product, nor would they alter their traditional patterns. All these things have kept Bijar carpets in demand in spite of the great quantity, variety and sophistication of carpets woven in the cities. To say that one is "better" than the other is like saying that orchestral music is "better" than folk music—they simply belong to different categories.

Plate 41, Bijar

Weavers in the village of Bijar are noted for their strong adherence to a tradition of making extremely sturdy and hard-wearing carpets, and for continuing to use natural dyes long after synthetic dyes had become widespread in Persia. The shape of this piece indicates that it was probably made for the local market. With the growth of exports to the West in the late nineteenth-century, Persian weavers were obliged to produce carpets with a squarer shape, better suited to the American living room. The complex design of this example, an 'arabesque' lattice filled with flowers, was produced by copying, most likely from a sample carpet (see the Bijar on page 15).

So how did the merchant entrepreneurs of Sultanabad tackle the problem of conveying the new patterns needed for the American market to the weavers? The approach was to take advantage of two techniques long known in both Persia and Turkey. The first of these makes use of the villager weavers' habit of copying. The merchants initially ordered a number of small sample carpets to be made. Each included a section of one or more field designs and often several border designs. These sample carpets were then given out by the merchants to weavers in the villages. By copying from these samples it was possible for them to weave the complete pattern for several different carpets by using the given sample patterns in a variety of combinations. These sample carpets are interesting in their own right and do occasionally appear on the market to the delight of a few dedicated collectors. They are called in the trade *vagireh*, an abbreviation of *farsh-e vagireh*, which in Persian means "copying carpet." The use of sample carpets for copying was not actually invented by the merchants of Sultanabad for the system was already in use in both Turkey and Persia. An example from the village of Bijar, shown right, which is for the field design only, makes an interesting comparison to the Bijar carpet, page 15.

The second technique for recording and distributing carpet designs is the squared-paper cartoon. Sadly, no carpet cartoons older than the nineteenth century have survived. However, by examining some old carpets in detail we can be sure that cartoons have been in use for at least four hundred years.

The whole system of making and using cartoons calls for some sophistication on the part of the weavers and the designers. In former times, cartoons were used only in situations where the greatest technological refinements were available, such as large workshops in the cities and the weaving establishments serving the royal courts.

The theory of the system of weaving from a cartoon is extremely simple. The vertical threads of the warp and the transverse threads of the weft form a grid and can be represented on a sheet of squared paper by the vertical and horizontal lines. As already mentioned the pattern of a carpet is built up knot by knot, line by line, beginning at one end and working through to the other. In a finished cartoon, one square on the paper corresponds to one knot of the carpet; the weaver builds up the carpet by following precisely the sequence of colored knots indicated in the cartoon.

In practice, there are several stages in the process of making a cartoon. First, an artist or designer makes a drawing on squared paper. In the times of the Shahs and Sultans of the sixteenth and seventeenth centuries, the artists who designed carpets for the court were men of high attainment. Some were scholars and poets as well as artists of international renown; and some were of such distinction that rulers in different countries would compete for their services. These days there are few rulers capable of extending such patronage, and the artist-designer is not so highly regarded. Even so the skills of the carpet designer survive, and in Iran today the craft is still practiced at a high level.

BIJAR

A copying carpet from Bijar, called vagireh in Persian. Sometimes copying carpets include more than one field design and several border designs. The weavers copy this instead of using a cartoon. A copied design is never as accurately reproduced as one woven from a cartoon, and when the copy is itself copied, the design becomes increasingly distorted. The naive irregularities in the design of this example indicate that many generations of copies lie between it and the original. (9' 1" x 5' 9") Photo: Sotheby's, New York

PLATE 53, TABRIZ, OPPOSITE

The complex lattice of branching arabesque tracery filled with flowers is similar in concept to that of the Bijar, page 15, though executed here with elegantly flowing curves and a much greater overall precision. In contrast to the Bijar, this carpet was woven from cartoons, one for the field — repeated in a series of flips sixteen times — and one for the border. The way main border pattern is constructed is easily seen at the ends. The unit of design is quite small and has been used in six horizontal flips, thus: ❦ ❧ ❦ ❧ ❦ ❧ For the side borders it has simply been turned at right angles. A grid has been drawn on the carpet to demonstrate.

PLATE 52, TABRIZ
A design of this complexity would be too difficult to memorize and would certainly have been woven from two cartoons, one for the field, and another for the border. The field pattern has been built up by horizontal and vertical flips of a single unit of design ⟨⟩ ⟨⟩ ⟨⟩ ⟨⟩ in the same way that tiles are laid to produce larger composite ⟨⟩ ⟨⟩ ⟨⟩ ⟨⟩ patterns. Here there are eight "tiles" in the center of the field and two "half tiles" at each end.

At the next stage, the artist's drawing is colored in. He may do it himself or he may have other craftsmen do it for him. There are two levels of skill in this operation. The less skilled of the two fills in the main blocks of color, beginning with the light colors and finishing with the dark. The more skilled fills in the outlines. This is extremely exacting work for both of them and very time-consuming since there are routinely nine or ten colors in a carpet, often fifteen, and sometimes more than twenty. When all the tiny squares have been colored in, the squared paper is cut up into sections of convenient size and pasted on to a stiff card or board, which may then be varnished.

Since the great revival of carpet weaving in the nineteenth century, the use of cartoons has become more widespread. These days, they are not only found in towns and cities, but are also used in villages and sometimes even by nomads. Whereas cartoons were formerly designed and made to order, in the cities today a whole new service sector has grown up dedicated to producing cartoons "off the peg" for sale to anyone looking for a new fashionable design to make at home (see page 23).

The pattern for a complete carpet will consist of a set of cartoons, the number depending on the complexity of the design. Just as tiles can be designed to make bigger patterns by placing four together, so carpet patterns can be built up by horizontal and vertical flips of the same pattern unit. For example, if we look at the Agra, page 22 (top right), the field design splits into two mirror-image halves. All the weaver would need is a cartoon for one half because in practice they begin at one edge and when they reach the middle they tie the same knots in reverse sequence. Now look carefully at the field design of the Tabriz, left. It consists of a single tile-like pattern unit repeated eight times, plus two half "tiles" at each end. Likewise, the field design of the Tabriz with the split-leaf lattice, page 16, is constructed from one quite small unit of design used sixteen times.

Here, the main border tells us something interesting. Take a look at the main border at one end. It consists of a single unit of design repeated six times in this manner: ⟨⟩ ⟨⟩ ⟨⟩ ⟨⟩ ⟨⟩ ⟨⟩

The weaver has then turned the cartoon through 90 degrees and continued using the design for the side borders in the same way. Now compare this border with that of the Agra carpet, page 22 (top left), in which the strap like arabesques continue round the main border, making a neat 45 degree transition in each corner. This orderly transition, seen also in the main border of the two Agra carpets, pages 21 and 22 (top right), is made possible by designing an extra cartoon specially for the corners. The corner cartoon is, of course, an extra expense and is used in carpets intended for the most demanding and sophisticated clientele.

The height of refinement and understated elegance is achieved in the Aubusson, page 22. Not only does it have "fully fashioned" corners, but each corner is different. Furthermore, the border, which at first sight appears rather uniform, has no repeat in it anywhere. Likewise, the central wreath,

The Eastern Carpet and the West

its little variations in direct contrast to the restrained austerity of the endlessly repeating field pattern, is not placed symmetrically on the background, nor is the background symmetrical in relation to the border. The whole ensemble provides a subtle and intentional artistic challenge to the senses.

Another ingenious and entirely different way of transmitting an artist's design to a weaver was invented in India and may have been used for one or more of the Agra carpets. It consists of a written instruction to the weaver specifying which colored knots to tie, how many of each, and in what sequence, for each row of knots in the carpet. The instruction is written in a special notation, like a knitting pattern. A weaver may work alone, reading the instruction from a strip of paper at the loom; however, a more efficient use of the system is to weave several carpets with the same pattern at the same time. In this situation, a master weaver calls out the colors to those working at the nearby looms in a special sing-song intonation so that everyone can hear.

Having solved the problem of transmitting designs to the weavers, the merchant-entrepreneurs intent on selling carpets to the West were faced with the dilemma that all commercial carpet producers have had to wrestle with ever since: What designs are going to be popular and sell well?

At first, carpets were made using designs already in circulation, and the ones that sold most quickly were produced in greatest quantity. But the designers were not content with this situation for long, and soon they began to look round for ways to increase their repertoire of patterns. At first they turned to the old carpets that were still in circulation and copied them, sometimes with great attention for accuracy. One such is the Agra shown on

The carpet-designer today is a specialist who devotes his skills entirely to carpets. This artist in Teheran is making a design on squared paper which will be colored in by someone else. We do not know exactly how carpet designs were produced in the past, but the artists had to be extremely versatile, since in addition to miniature paintings and book illuminations, they were called on to produce designs in many media—textiles, woodwork, stonework decoration, even ceramics.

The artist's drawing is colored in by another specialist, seen working here in Teheran. Each colored square represents one knot of the carpet. Even though the background color is left blank, the work is demanding and enormously time-consuming. The design for one quarter of the carpet is nearing completion. When finished, the cartoon will be cut up into numbered sections of manageable size which are pasted onto a board and then protected by a coat of varnish.

The proprietor of a supervised workshop near Na'in which specializes in making very fine carpets, keeps a tight control on the amount of wool used by the sixteen girls he employs. He avoids waste by handing out a small quantity of each color only when it is needed.

This girl is using a cartoon to knot the main border design of a large and extremely fine Na'in carpet on which eight people are working. Weavers are paid according to their level of skill: the more skilled know how to work the designs from a cartoon, and the less skilled fill in the plain areas in between.

page 22 (top left) and plate 61, which has been copied from a seventeenth-century Persian carpet. The original design is somewhat more complicated, but the pattern may have been modified intentionally for reasons of economy.[1]

About this time western interest in carpets, both old and new, was growing fast. A number of exhibitions were held and some lavish volumes published with illustrations of the best surviving antique examples. These books were seized on by designers looking for new ideas. Some of the illustrated carpets were reproduced in their entirety, but it is difficult to capture the spirit of something without seeing it, and these copies are generally unsatisfactory. More often the old design schemes were reinterpreted using different colors—the Agra carpet, right, is a good example of this treatment. The original design for this carpet is known in only two surviving pieces: one in the Musée Historique des Tissus in Lyon and the other in the Metropolitan Museum of Art in New York. Both date from the sixteenth century and are magnificent examples of the art of Persian carpet weaving. The Agra version is much simplified and has an intentionally restrained color scheme; nevertheless, the dragons and phoenixes present in the original are there, and the sense of a pattern repeating endlessly and extending out beneath the border is also retained.

When carpets began to be traded in the West, buyers were at first happy to indulge their taste for the exotic and enjoyed having something from a foreign culture in their living rooms. Even so, some colors were preferred over others, and the sellers in America took great pains to provide what people wanted, even to the point of bleaching out the color from some carpets and re-tinting them in a more desirable shade.

On the other hand, there was an established western taste in interior decorating that followed European fashions, and in the late nineteenth century the demand for European-style furnishing carpets was still strong. The fashion at that time was for large floral patterns on a dark blue or black background, and importers in Europe and America let the producers know that not only were new sizes required to suit Western demand but some European-style designs would be popular too. The producers, always keen to please their customers, began to produce designs reflecting the fashionable European taste of the period. At first the demand came mainly from Russia, and the Karabagh carpet (the region of Karabagh came within the Russian cultural sphere in the second half of the nineteenth century), with its large

PLATE 62, AGRA
The design of this carpet is a rather free interpretation of an early sixteenth century Persian original. These carpets became known to designers after the publication of some of the best surviving examples of the art of the knotted-pile carpet around the turn of the century. It too has accurately designed corners.

PLATE 61, AGRA

Carpet designers are always on the look-out for ideas, and carpets from the past have long been a source of inspiration. This carpet is an accurate copy of a seventeenth century Persian carpet, though the original was longer and had a slightly more complicated design.

PLATE 71, AGRA

In contrast to the Tabriz, page 18, the border design of this carpet turns through forty-five degrees to make a neat transition between the vertical and the horizontal. This indicates that an additional cartoon was made for the corners—an extra expense. As there is only a single mirror-image repeat in the field design, the weavers would have had to work from a rather large cartoon covering half the entire field —also expensive. The extra time and labor involved in this work indicates that it was made for an up-market clientele.

LEFT: PLATE 92, AUBUSSON

The apparent simplicity of the design of this French, tapestry-woven carpet is deceptive. There are subtleties everywhere that only reveal themselves when one starts to look carefully. For example all the corners are different and nowhere in the border does the simple flower pattern repeat itself. The understatement is intentional; such pieces were designed for a discerning clientele.

wreath like design decorated with cabbage roses, is typical of the European-influenced patterns of that period (see plate number 86, in *The Collection*.) It is interesting that this style has come back into fashion recently to such an extent that a century later similar designs are once more being produced.

SINCE THOSE TIMES, fashions in interior decorating have come and gone, and all the producing countries have been through economic ups and downs. In spite of the inevitable changes that occur with the passing of time, the techniques and methods for producing carpets today remain the same as they were a hundred years ago. The knots are still tied by hand, and the process is as labor-intensive as it ever was. The main change has been in the organization of production—an extension of the process begun by the merchants of Sultanabad in the 1870s. The local designers are still trying to guess what their western clients will like, but now they have been joined by a corps of designers based in the West, principally America. These western designers use computers to generate what are called "programmed lines'" in which a single design is adapted to different shapes and sizes. Contracts for producing carpets in these designs are then placed by the US-based companies with one of the numerous workshops specializing in fulfilling such orders that have grown up in various countries, including India, Pakistan, Turkey, China, and Egypt.

The result of this new arrangement is that buyers in America do not have to go to a rug store to buy, they can now choose a suitable carpet from a catalog, since each design is available in five or six different sizes. This is an efficient and effective way of both producing and marketing, and it removes the temptation to reduce the length or width of a rug to fit a particular space—a fate that has befallen many large pieces in the past. But in raising standards and increasing the range of the product are we not in danger of losing the very thing that is so attractive about the art of carpets—the sense that every piece has an individual character? What can match the naive charm of the Agra carpet, shown on page 23 and plate 71, with its riot of birds and animals dashing, lurking, roosting, or simply hiding in the fantastic foliage of their other-worldly forest? But I must not let my nostalgia get the better of me, lest one morning I wake up to find a catalog in the mail offering a new range of carpets called something like 'Fabulous Forest,' with that very same Agra design in ten different shapes and sizes!

A carpet-making supplies shop in Isfahan sells balls of white cotton yarn for the warp, colored wools for the pile, beating combs, small frame-looms and cartoons. On the right is a six-cartoon set for the field design of a medium-sized carpet, and next to it a three-cartoon set for a small rug. The border designs are sold separately. The time taken to draw and color in the cartoons makes them expensive, but they last a long time and can be exchanged among friends and family.

Footnote
1. The original for this design is seen in the carpet illustrated in Christie's London, Nov. 11 1993, lot 106.

The Collection

Late 19th-Century Mahal

20' x 12' (6.09 x 3.66 m)

Persia

———◊———

THE DESIGNS OF THE ROSETTES at each end of the piece are virtually identical, but the way their several parts are colored makes them appear totally different. The field contains many other examples of this shrewd color substitution technique. The field so entrances that one is unaware of the small size of the basic design from which it has been derived. The success of such sleight of hand requires consummate skill on the part of the designer. This rarely utilized technique is analogous to the use of "theme and variations" in musical compositions.

The elegance of this masterly design is not confined to its field; it is also evident in the slim, dark blue border with its ivory-colored inner and outer guards.

The finished carpet is all the more praiseworthy for being so subtle and understated. In this, the designer has been especially well served both by the weavers and by the wool dyers, whose colors are still as vibrant and alive as the day the carpet was cut down from its loom.

Plate 1

The tomato-red field has a column of salmon pink and pale apricot-hued medallions, flowerheads, and arabesques surrounded by palmettes and flowering vines. It is contained within an indigo border of feathery palmettes and flowering vines, between ivory-colored and brick-red floral stripes.

Late 19th-Century Ziegler

20' 5" x 12' 4" (6.22 x 3.76 m)

Persia

Ziegler carpets dominated the market from the late 19th century until the first world war, after which their primacy was challenged and, eventually, overtaken by a huge increase in Tabriz production. It is only in the last decade or so that discriminating buyers have realized that their ancestors (skipping one generation, perhaps two) were right to find so much contentment in these beautiful but unpretentious carpets.

Great skill was employed in the design studios to make the carpets appear simultaneously modern and traditional. Their success can be gauged by contemplating this particular example, which was likely woven for an American client (Europeans tended to prefer sizes as large as 14 feet by 11 feet). The design is simplicity itself: the artist created a small section in his studio, and the rest was done at the loom by rotation about the vertical axis and, once that band was complete, by rotation about the horizontal axis.

The dark blue of the medallions is taken up in the border color, which has a traditional pattern of palmettes connected by meandering leaves.

The pattern works wonderfully, for the carpet is very nicely balanced in appearance and has great strength and dignity.

Plate 2

The shaded tomato-red field has a central column of indigo cruciform medallions surrounded by large olive-green radiating medallions and minor palmettes and flowering vines. It is contained within an indigo palmette and feathery leafy vine border, between pale apricot-hued floral stripes.

Late 19th-Century Mahal

16' 4" x 11' (4.98 x 3.35 m)

Persia

———·◇·———

THE STRANGE AND WONDERFUL THING about carpets from Persia is the seeming never-ending variety of their designs. No two carpets are ever the same—although certain similar characteristics are often identifiable, as in this fine Mahal.

In this case, the well-established style—multilineal borders framing an excitingly designed center—echoes a familiar Persian format. Yet, what an intricate design it is!

Recognized universally as one of the world's great carpet centers, this particular Mahal lives up to its reputation. It is of consistently high quality and vibrant coloring, but still achieves an atmosphere of (almost) forgotten charm.

Plate 3

The shaded brick-red field with ivory- and pale apricot-colored palmette medallions is surrounded by flowering vines. It is contained within an indigo border of turtle-palmettes and flowering vines, between ivory-colored flowering vines and reciprocal Y-pattern stripes.

Late 19th-Century Sultanabad

15' 5" x 10' (4.70 x 3.05 m)

Persia

FEW EQUALED, AND NONE BETTERED, the heavenly light blues to be found in Sultanabad work. Many dealers use the presence of this blue as their principal criterion for attributing a rug to that area. As this particular blue vanished around the turn of the century, never to be rivaled, it is also useful in dating. The copper-colored field is equally lovely and is typical of the genre, although, in this case, it is still extant.

This carpet uses a mirror image design rather than one laid out in horizontal bands. The *abradjs* at each end of the field, though barely apparent, help to break up the repetitious nature of this sort of allover design, and thus contribute positively to the carpet's overall appeal.

Plate 4

The shaded rust-red field has a central column of stylized vases issuing flowering leafy sprays, flanked by stylized cypress trees and floral sprays. It is contained within a pale blue palmette and vine border, between ivory-colored flowering vine stripes.

Late 19th-Century Mahal

14' 10" x 11' (4.52 x 3.35 m)

Persia

ONLY IN RECENT YEARS has there been a documented appreciation of the extent and nature of 19th-century European influence on the production of carpets in central Persia. One reputed type is known by the name of its manufacturer, the British firm of Ziegler & Co. Other companies, however, were also busy in the province of Arak, and they supplied largely similar goods in a wide range of qualities to the same markets.

This carpet is a fine example of a piece from one of these other firms. It is well made with good wool on a warp and weft of excellent cotton. The pleasing allover design has many interesting minor motifs scattered in an orderly manner across the cream-colored field.

While the field is essentially curvilinear, the sophisticated, dark blue border shows the stricter disciplines of the rectilinear mode. The rich and vibrant colors of the carpet have survived miraculously to the present day.

Plate 5

The ivory-colored field has columns of radiating flowerheads and palmettes and vines surrounded by feathery leaves. It is contained within an indigo border of palmettes and feathery leafy vines, between pale apricot-hued and pale yellow flowering vine stripes, with an inner reciprocal Y-pattern stripe.

Late 19th-Century Bakshayesh

14' 8" x 9' 6" (4.47 x 2.90 m)

Persia

WHOEVER SAID the language of art is universal had not seen this carpet!

Made in Persia at the end of the 19th century, this very special Bakshayesh displays myriad orderly symbols, yet they are not readily interpreted. They might represent a thousand stars in a midnight sky perhaps, or even glowing candles in a garden setting. The colors of this carpet are also inspiring. Is the center a midnight sky and the border a sunlit garden?.

The interpretation is entirely subjective. Whatever the meaning, though, the effect is fabulous, and we can only wonder at the magical touch of the craftsmen who made such a work of art.

Plate 6

The shaded indigo field has columns of midbrown and ivory-colored, serrated; stylized cypress trees surrounded by angular, stylized flowering vines and perching birds. It is contained within a broad ivory-colored border of angular, brick-red tracery vines and large, multicolored palmettes, between brick-red flowering vines and reciprocal skittle-pattern stripes.

Late 19th Century Sultanabad

14' 7" x 9' 10" (4.44 x 3 m)

PERSIA

IT IS NOT AT ALL UNUSUAL for a Persian carpet to feature all manner of animals and birds in its field and borders. It is very unusual indeed, however, to come across a totally nonrepresentational field with a border design containing birds and animals. Such designs are rare and apparently occur when the detail of the field has been imposed upon a designer but he has been allowed free rein in executing the border.

This carpet is such an example. It has a regular allover field, but features animals in the border. On closer examination, we begin to notice the designer's subtle sense of humor. He uses alternating pairs of animals: a pair of spring lambs gamboling over a small hillock and a pair of bears apparently deep in conversation. Are they discussing the quality of the local nuts, the recent weather, or merely on how they should bring up their cubs?

PLATE 7

The ivory-colored field has a central column of pale yellow, brick-red, and ivory- and apricot-colored medallions and lozenges surrounded by similar minor motifs and feathery vines. It is contained within a shaded brick-red border of palmettes and feathery leafy vines and a wide variety of animals, between ivory-colored and blue floral stripes.

Late 19th-Century Sultanabad

14' 5" x 13' 5" (4.39 x 4.09 m)

Persia

———— ·◇· ————

THE AMAZING THING about this carpet from Sultanabad is its extraordinary vivacity. It is perfectly symmetrical—balanced in coloring, motif, and layout—yet manages never to be dull.

The border alone gives the impression of jewels in an elaborate necklace. The central feature of the entire composition, however, is the strict adhesion to form. Rare to say the least, this carpet is exciting in every respect.

Plate 8

The ivory-colored field has an overall design of massive floral palmettes surrounded by arabesques and flowering vines. It is contained within a broad indigo border of red, yellow, and olive-green concentric medallions surrounded by flowering vines and floral sprays, between ivory-colored and red, serrated and flowering vines and plain stripes.

LATE 19TH-CENTURY BAKSHAYESH

14' x 11' 4" (4.27 x 3.45 m)

PERSIA

THE INFINITE VARIETY OF DESIGNS found in fine carpets the world over is remarkable. But of all nations, Persia is unequalled for its vast array of offerings.

This large Bakshayesh has a glorious, eye-popping design, with colors so varied and harmonious that one marvels at the sheer melody of the design.

Symmetrical to the point of extreme precision, the dancing forms nevertheless put one in mind of a graceful ballet in which we, too, enter the realm of fantasy the weaver has created.

This Bakshayesh is a prime example of fine carpets as a legitimate art form.

PLATE 9

The shaded fox-brown field with staggered rows of multicolored stylized plants is contained within a brick-red border of stylized floral roundels surrounded by angular, serrated vines, between pale apricot-hued and blue flowerhead stripes, serrated, and plain golden outer stripes.

Late 19th-Century Mahal

14' x 10' 8" (4.27 x 3.25 m)

PERSIA

———◊———

NO GREAT KNOWLEDGE IS NEEDED to appreciate works of art, merely observation and patience. This is perhaps the greatest joy of art appreciation—that all that is needed is the capacity to be charmed and to have the quality of one's life affected by the artist's work.

This Mahal is a fine example of the power of art to affect the onlooker. Even allowing for personal preferences, the quality of the design, form, and color blend so harmoniously in this carpet that one can truly call it a fine example of the artistry possible when a weaver is working at the very pinnacle of his profession.

Plate 10

The shaded ivory-colored field has columns of multicolored palmettes surrounded by flowering tendrils and other palmettes. It is contained within a shaded brick-red palmette and feathery, leafy vine border, between apricot- and pale olive-hued floral stripes and reciprocal inner Y-pattern stripe.

Late 19th-Century Bakshayesh

14' x 10' 5" (4.27 x 3.18 m)

Persia

NOMADIC TRIBES furnished their tents with carpets for practical reasons, with the best rugs only brought out for special guests. However, carpets in permanent locations probably began to appear when wandering peoples settled in villages and towns. At this time, temples, too, probably began to be similarly embellished.

This particular Persian carpet from Bakshayesh embodies most of the traditional qualities of the historic genre. Its coloring especially identifies it, along with numerous motifs, including flowers and stars linked by the almost invisible "thread of time." Framed by unbroken borders of linked flowers, the simplicity of the concept masks the underlying motive—namely, perfect congruity in design, form, and execution.

Plate 11

The shaded brick-red field has an overall design of cypress trees surrounded by angular flowering vines with perching birds and palmettes and floral sprays. It is contained within a light blue border of palmettes and serrated leafy vines, between indigo and ivory-colored flowerhead stripes.

Late 19th-Century Sultanabad

13' 10" x 9' (4.22 x 2.74 m)

PERSIA

———— ·◊· ————

THE INVENTIVENESS OF THE WEAVER is everything in carpet design. Flowers and other symbols play their part in the overall design, but the form the carpet will take comes from the weaver's imagination.

In this Sultanabad, we see many of the motifs favored by Persian designers; coloring, too, is typical of the genre. But what is unusual are the seven-fold, lineal borders, each with its own distinctive symbols. Florets, stars, and linked ribbons complete a picture of intense activity that never gets out of the control of the talented weaver who executed this carpet.

The result is a true work of genius.

PLATE 12

The blood-red field has stylized cypress trees and large flowering plants, contained within an indigo palmette, flowerhead, and flowering vine border, between ivory-, indigo-, and apricot-colored flowering vine stripes.

LATE 19TH-CENTURY ZIEGLER

13' 5" x 7' 8" (4.09 x 2.34 m)

PERSIA

ONE CAN IMAGINE this carpet in dozens of beautiful settings—from the palatial to the homey. Coloring enhances the dancing flowers—as if a summer breeze wafted through a meadow and set the whole ensemble in motion.

There is nothing static or contrived in this design. No jarring motifs seem out of place in the composition. This carpet makes one feel that all is right with the world. If only all things were a fraction as beautiful, then heaven would not be far away after all.

PLATE 13

The shaded brick-red field has a central column of steel-gray, radiating palmette medallions surrounded by golden, hooked flowering vines, olive-green radiating flowerheads, and stylized flowering vines. It is contained within a golden border of palmettes and vines, between yellow and red flowering vine stripes.

Late 19th-Century Ziegler

13' 4" x 11' 7" (4.06 x 3.53 m)

Persia

———— ·◊· ————

This Sultanabad displays enormous confidence and vigor. At its center is a floral design as beautifully executed as any by a fine artist, while the massive border, decorated with what appear to be scarabs and florets, displays considerable style and artistry.

In the right setting, this carpet would command a great deal of attention.

Plate 14

The tomato-red field has a central column of ivory-colored, serrated palmettes, surrounded by shaded indigo palmettes and shaded golden floral sprays, themselves surrounded by minor floral sprays. It is contained within a broad indigo border of ivory-colored and pale olive-green, angular flowering vines, surrounded by minor flowerheads, between ivory-colored and olive-green, stylized flowering vine stripes with inner reciprocal stripe.

LATE 19TH-CENTURY ZIEGLER

13' 4" x 9' 10" (4.06 x 3 m)

PERSIA

CLASSICAL INTERIORS have never lost their appeal. Certain variations on the classical theme come and go, but the firmly established format has hardly varied in 200 years.

This is particularly true in Europe, where all carpets of the classical mode were referred to as "Persian." Any differentiation was known only to experts and to the very enlightened.

Things are different now, though. The advent of interior design as an art form and the greater number of people knowledgeable about carpets have worked miracles. Classical carpets remain very much in demand.

This Persian carpet is a perfect example of the classical genre. Its very coloring underlines the "less is more" principle appreciated by so many carpet lovers. Such muted colors belong to that age of elegance that many deem to be a thing of the past, but which this wonderful carpet assures us is not so.

PLATE 15

The pale shaded yellow field has a central column of palmettes and feathery leaves surrounded by similar palmettes and flowering vines. It is contained within a broad indigo palmette and vine border, between shaded brick-red and ivory-colored flowering vine stripes.

LATE 19TH-CENTURY ZIEGLER

13' 2" x 7' 8" (4.01 x 2.34 m)

PERSIA

PARTLY BECAUSE OF the lack of comparable specimens, interior designers in the 19th century often chose "safe" Persian designs in the full knowledge that their clients had few ideas of their own. There must have been exceptions, but, by and large, important town houses were accustomed to seeing fine "Persian" rugs in their various rooms.

In the 20th century, however, things are very different. Both designers and clients are usually well informed and exercise their personal judgments as to what is preferable in a specific location.

Conflicts seldom arise, but preferences are acknowledged. This fine Ziegler carpet, with its wonderful perspective, would never be used in any setting but one of importance. Discreetly beautiful, it would be ideal as an entrance hall adornment or for use in a corridor. In its own right, it is both artistic and sumptuous.

PLATE 16

The shaded indigo field has a central column of palmettes, flowerheads, and turtle-palmettes, in a tomato-red turtle-palmette border of angular flowering vines, between pale blue and golden flowering vines and reciprocal stripes, and plain outer indigo stripe.

LATE 19TH-CENTURY ZIEGLER

12' 9" x 9' 2" (3.89 x 2.79 m)

PERSIA

———⋄———

IT IS REMARKABLE how Persian artisans continue to astound us with their inventiveness and never-ending masterpieces.

This terric Ziegler carpet is a particularly fine example of the Persian skill in arranging objects, symbols, and angles into a pleasing combination. Framed by a traditional arrangement of florets and linked ribbons, the carpet presents a beautiful ensemble of just about every kind of usual pattern variation. The effect is riveting.

PLATE 17

The ivory-colored field has three columns of open, radiating, brick-red and light blue medallions surrounded by minor, stylized flowerheads and floral sprays. It is contained within an indigo turtle-palmette and stylized flowering vine border, between tomato-red flowering vines and reciprocal Y-pattern stripes.

LATE 19TH-CENTURY ZIEGLER

12' 8" x 10' 6" (3.86 x 3.20 m)

PERSIA

THIS SPECTACULAR SULTANABAD seems on first impression to be in the classical mode. Closer inspection, however, reveals that the pattern is an explosive one—with the design fragmenting into a jigsaw of intriguing symbols. There are so many eye-popping elements in this carpet that its full meaning cannot be taken in with one glance.

As one looks farther at the intensity of the design, it becomes obvious that there is order and control in the execution. The regularity of the surrounding border effectively contains the great activity found within the center panel, and the strict formality of the smaller borders show deference to classical design.

PLATE 18

The steel blue field has an overall design of stylized ivory and apricot palmettes, tendrils, flowers and vine, in a broad shaded brick-red palmette and flowering vine border, between ivory flowering vine stripes with a plain blue outer stripe.

LATE 19TH-CENTURY ZIEGLER

12' x 9' (3.66 x 2.74 m)

PERSIA

ALL HOMES CAN BENEFIT from the presence of a happy carpet, and this pretty Mahal satisfies perfectly on that point. Not a single element jars the senses. It is in every respect a joy to behold.

Flowers and stars and leaves and ribbons are all set within traditional borders. The warm earth tones also inspire in the beholder a feeling of liveliness, joy, and happiness.

This carpet is an enchanting example of an artifact that fulfills its basic purpose yet goes far beyond. Some carpets are imperial, some are merely grand; this Ziegler is simply beautiful.

PLATE 19

The shaded rust-red field has a lattice of palmettes, floral medallions, flowerheads, and feathery leaves. It is contained within an indigo turtle-palmette and flowering vine border, between multiple, ivory-colored flowering vines and mill-pattern stripes.

Late 19th-Century Mahal

12' 3" x 9' 10" (3.73 x 3 m)

Persia

FINE CARPETS are an artistic and practical way to enliven a home. This colorful Mahal carpet is an excellent choice.

Renowned for their unique designs, Mahal carpets are also recognized internationally for their quality and vitality.

This particular example has a classically laid-out border that uses a format established in ancient times. It is not a slavish imitation of other carpets, however, for every carpet worthy of the Mahal name makes a unique statement in both design and format. The allegiance to classicism is much admired and sought after, but the individual interpretation of that allegiance is the important issue.

This unique Mahal does exactly that.

Plate 20

The shaded rust-red field has a lattice of blue, pink, ivory-colored, and brown palmette medallions and flowerheads. It is contained within an indigo turtle-palmette and flowering vine border, between very floral and reciprocal Y-pattern stripes.

LATE 19TH-CENTURY ZIEGLER

12' x 8' 4" (3.66 x 2.54 m)

PERSIA

HERE IS ANOTHER imaginative Ziegler.

The carpet is vibrant and exciting, has an intriguing design, and is decorated with such flair that it deserves a second look. The strict geometric layout was no accident of design, but a carefully modulated piece of precision.

Decorated with regional symbols, this carpet is in no way a naive piece of weaver's workmanship, but a distinctive work of art.

PLATE 21

The shaded rust-red field has a counterposed design of ivory- and aubergine-colored palmettes and tracery vines with feathery leaves. It is contained within a shaded aubergine-colored border of palmettes and angular vines, between double floral and Y-pattern stripes.

LATE 19TH-CENTURY HERIZ

11' 5" x 8' 3" (3.48 x 2.51 m)

PERSIA

———·◇·———

LATE IN THE 20TH CENTURY, there persists a deep nostalgia for the artistic traditions of the past. This is equally true when it comes to fine carpets. Traditional carpet styles are now much sought after by collectors and designers alike.

This noble Heriz is a prime example. Its many attributes—including motif, color, design, and size—appeal instantly to the modern eye. At home in both contemporary and classical settings, it has a universal appeal and charm.

In addition, this Heriz is a classic example of its genre. The design of linked ribbons encompassing flags and florets, set within the traditional border, is instantly recognizable and much valued by experts.

PLATE 22

The tomato-red field has a lattice of indigo radiating flowerheads and palmettes surrounded by stylized flowering vines. It is contained within a border of indigo flowerheads and angular serrated vines, between reciprocal floral stripes and inner blue cruciform stripes.

LATE 19TH-CENTURY ZIEGLER

11' 3" x 8' 4" (3.43 x 2.54 m)

PERSIA

THE ELABORATE DESIGN of this magnificent Ziegler inspires awe. Wherever one looks, there are eye-catching design motifs. The carpet is so complex, it is almost impossible to isolate individual elements and attempt to decipher the meaning of the pattern.

Such a carpet cannot help but dominate its surroundings. Paired with fine furniture, however, it will more than hold its own. No matter what setting it is placed in, this fabulous carpet will seem perfectly at home.

PLATE 23

The ivory-colored field has a large olive-green, serrated-leaf lattice enclosing palmettes, flowerheads, and flowering vines. It is contained within a broad indigo border of palmettes and angular, stylized flowering vines, between blue and steel-gray boteh vine stripes.

Late 19th-Century Mahal

10' 6" x 8' 5" (3.20 x 2.57 m)

Persia

———·∽·———

This fine Mahal carpet, with its high-quality design, exudes extravagance and cries out for a setting of luxury and privilege.

It was designed to complement a rich interior and add color and fascination to its surroundings. With one glance, one is assured that this special carpet was destined to fulfill a rich man's dream. It would be out of place anywhere else. Some treasures may only belong to the man who can afford them.

Plate 24

The shaded tomato red field has a large ivory-colored lattice enclosing palmettes and flowerheads. It is contained within a broad, ivory-colored turtle-palmette and angular, stylized vine border, between ivory-colored and olive-green floral stripes.

Late 19th-Century Sultanabad

10' 4" x 7' 9" (3.15 x 2.36 m)

Persia

Developed over centuries and evolved to a high art form, Persian carpets set the standard by which all great carpets are measured. Just one look at a Persian carpet recalls an era when highly skilled weavers worked with patrons to achieve a perfect combination of design excellence, careful craftsmanship, and unique personal expression.

The regional location of this rare Sultanabad evokes fantasies of great palaces and mosques. The swirling arabesques and esoteric motifs establish a design pattern that holds the attention, even as one struggles to understand its meaning. In complete contrast, the surrounding border is designed within strictly formal guidelines, leaving an impression of severity and beauty. This is deliberate, of course, for nothing about these great carpets is ever haphazard.

The overall effect is of lively challenge and sumptuous elegance. A rare combination indeed.

Plate 25

The shaded indigo field has a central column of pale apricot-hued and indigo medallions surrounded by flowerheads and floral palmettes and floral sprays. It is contained within a brick-red border of palmettes and vine, between ivory-colored angular flowering vine stripes.

Late 19th-Century Mahal

10' 4" x 6' 8" (3.15 x 2.03 m)

PERSIA

Muted colors and classical formats became synonymous with the houses of well-to-do families in the 19th century. Nothing was ever allowed to jar the eye or offend the prevailing sensibility of good taste and breeding.

This fine Mahal would have been at home in all the great town houses of the wealthy—from London to Boston, Paris to New York.

Little has changed. Such clients today might demand a wider choice, somewhat more adventurous carpets, but by and large taste has not altered appreciably. Why change, when the centuries have proven the success of such a formula?

In this Mahal, one sees both conformity and a small concession to a new expressionism, as seen in the center motifs with their unusual configurations. The colors and surrounding borders conform wonderfully, but the hint of change apparent here makes for a very interesting carpet.

Plate 26

The tomato-red field has a column of massive, shaded brown and steel-gray palmettes and stylized flowerheads, surrounded by stylized flowering vines. It is contained within an indigo turtle-palmette and angular flowering vine border, between indigo- and apricot-hued flowering vine stripes and inner reciprocal Y-pattern stripes.

LATE 19TH-CENTURY ZIEGLER

9' 2" x 8' 6" (2.74 x 2.59 m)

PERSIA

A VERY FINE ADAPTATION of the *harshang* (or crab) design, in which the indentations of the large, soft rose-colored motifs are of birds' heads, all with open beaks. This extraordinary use of the tips of the flowers goes back many centuries and had all but died out by the 19th century. It is normally only found in the finer grades of Tabriz rugs and carpets, in the silk rugs of that area, and those that are described as Heriz in the international rug trade.

Carpets using this harshang design are often heavy in appearance but, because the motifs are spaced well apart and are predominantly in soft pastel colors, this particular piece manages to be light and airy.

The border is fashioned in the traditional Feraghan design, and its somewhat bolder colors reinforce the visual impact of its containing function.

PLATE 27

The pale yellow field has an overall design of columns of shaded brick-red, light blue, and caramel-colored concentric medallions surrounded by minor, similar medallions. It is contained within a broad, brick-red border of turtle-palmettes and vines, with an inner, light blue floral vine stripe.

LATE 19TH-CENTURY MESHED

22' 2" x 12' 6" (6.76 x 3.81 m)

PERSIA

DESIGNERS OF BOTH Khorassan and Isfahan are particularly enamored of the swirling line of an arabesque; yet, only the former are able to use it discreetly enough that its presence is not immediately evident. The object of the line is to compartmentalize, unify, and discipline what would otherwise be an amorphous riot of flowers.

This carpet is the work of a very skilled weaver. The swirling lines don't cease at the boundaries of the medallion or at the corners. On the contrary, they are echoed inside these, and their existence permits the use of a far greater number of flowers throughout.

Persians love flowers, experiencing in Nature's springtime bounty a *joie de vivre* at the birth of each bud and an inevitable sorrow, just weeks later, as the flower fades and becomes a distant memory. By weaving flower motifs into a carpet, these romantic souls capture the beauty and joy associated with flowers and offer those most fragile of God's creations immortality.

PLATE 28

The shaded blood-red field has a mass of palmettes and curling flowering vines around a large ivory-colored and indigo cusped and concentric, similar medallion, with similar spandrels. It is contained within an ivory-colored palmette and arabesque border, between multiple ivory-colored floral stripes.

LATE 19TH-CENTURY TABRIZ

21'8" x 12'8" (6.60 x 3.86 m)

PERSIA

———— ◈ ————

THE IMMEDIATE SURPRISE in this Tabriz is the intricacy of the design. Endless geometric progressions move in seemingly endless formations. Wherever one's attention wanders, some new path of exploration opens up.

Even the central medallion itself is set within another, which is also encompassed by a walled garden! Or, perhaps, they are not flowers but an army of warriors? Are the four corners guardian outposts or guards overseeing the vast central arena?

A more complex arrangement of motifs would be difficult to imagine, but the visual magnificence of the whole ensemble commands attention.

Something as beautiful as this carpet never comes about by chance. Furthermore, the geometric perfection rules out the notion of an experiment. The calculated precision of the design has about it the appeal of a mathematical formula, not readily decipherable, but eternally tantalizing.

PLATE 29

The indigo field has a Herati pattern around a similar cusped and scalloped ivory-colored central medallion. It is contained within a shaded brick-red similar frame, in an indigo turtle-palmette and flowering vine border, between multiple meandering vines and palmettes and serrated left stripes.

Late 19th-Century Tabriz

21' 4" x 13' 10" (6.50 x 4.22 m)

Persia

CARPETS AS BIG AS THIS ONE were always commissioned—never made in the hope that one day a buyer might appear. This meant that the work had to be undertaken with care and precision. The size would have been decided first, followed by a discussion of which of several designs should be employed for the various parts of the carpet. The next step would have been for the person commissioning the work to discuss the exact shade of each color he or she wished employed. There would have been much discussion about the quality of the materials to be used, then lengthy negotiations to obtain the finest knotting consistent with the depth of the buyer's purse. Finally, there may well have been argument about what we, nowadays, call "quality control." The caliber of the finished carpet depended exclusively on the correct amount of care being put into the initial order.

This handsome example of a Herati carpet reflects how hard earlier generations had to work to satisfy the buyer. There is, in this carpet, an unrivaled feeling for balance in overall design, details, and the harmony of colors. Usually, pieces that are based on the so-called Herati design have this pattern woven right through from border to border, with the corners and the medallion being distinguished by a change in the ground color. In this prestigious piece, one notes that the design is smaller in the very simple, cream ground medallions and in the inner border than in the field.

This border is traditionally associated with the so-called Herati patterned field. Its presence symbolizes great strength and the peace that arises from its proper use.

Carpets of this nature have always been popular with persons in authority because of the carpets' great dignity. Althought they exude an aura of power and self-assurance, they do so in a manner that is all the more effective for being understated.

Plate 30

The shaded tomato-red field has a fine overall floral tracery, comprising light blue flowerheads, indigo medallions, and feathery vines around a large, ivory-colored, scalloped and cusped medallion with Herati pattern, within a similar frame. It is contained within a shaded brick-red border of turtle-palmettes and flowering vines, between pale brown similar stripes.

LATE 19TH-CENTURY TABRIZ

21' x 14' 9" (6.40 x 4.50 m)

PERSIA

NOT EVEN THE ARRIVAL of the 20th century could change or even influence the creator(s) of this very special Tabriz. The subject matter, design, and coloring of this carpet pay homage to earlier times.

This carpet could easily have come from the 18th century. It is easy to imagine it in almost any palatial setting. That it will probably continue its journey in a modern interior is an exciting and enviable prospect.

The very scale of the carpet—21 feet by 14 feet 9 inches—marks it as monumental. Discreetly beautiful, elaborate yet immediately comprehensible, it pleases the eye and enchants the mind.

PLATE 31

The rust-red field has palmettes and floral sprays around a large indigo and ivory-colored similar medallion with pendants, within an indigo palmette and flowering vine frame with large ivory-colored floral medallions. It is contained within a shaded rust-red border of palmettes and flowering vines, between indigo and blue floral stripes and plain outer stripe.

LATE 19TH-CENTURY TABRIZ

18' 6" x 13' 8" (5.64 x 4.17 m)

PERSIA

———— ⋅◇⋅ ————

THIS MAGNIFICENT CARPET fully expresses the vitality and extraordinary artistry of Persia and speaks volumes about Persian sovereignty.

In equal measure, the color, design, and symbolism of this Tabriz reflect a nation unlike any in the world.

Whoever owns this masterpiece is merely a "custodian" of one of the art works of a nation.

PLATE 32

The shaded apricot-hued field has palmettes and floral sprays around a large cusped and indented dark brown floral medallion with palmettes and flower-heads, pendants, and similar spandrels. It is contained within a broad, shaded charcoal-gray border of palmettes and feathery leafy vines, between triple floral stripes and plain outer stripe.

Late 19th-Century Tabriz

17' 10" x 11' (5.44 x 3.35 m)

Persia

This pretty Tabriz, with its compelling sense of form and wonderful controlled design and coloring, underscores why Persia dominates the field of fine carpets.

Viewed from any angle, not a single misplaced or inappropriate motif interrupts the harmony of this carpet. Soft colors are used to great effect for the variously shaded symbols. The weaver used a delicacy of touch that is breathtaking. One is left with a final impression of beauty and understatement—a rare combination in any art form.

Plate 33

The ivory-colored field has palmettes and flowering vines around a large, central, cusped, and radiating pale olive-green floral medallion, with brick-red palmettes. It is contained within a shaded brick-red border of palmettes, flowerheads, and flowering vines, between pale green flowering vine stripes.

Late 19th-Century Tabriz

17' 4" x 12' 4" (5.28 x 3.76 m)

PERSIA

COMPARED WITH DESIGNS of more romantic appeal, this entrancing Tabriz seizes the imagination in quite a different way from any other carpet. Its power is almost hypnotic.

The emphasis on architectural nobility suggests this carpet belongs in a magnificent, even monumental, building of international acclaim—perhaps an embassy or the grand entrance to a classical museum. Whatever its setting, one would never be able to ignore it. Its tremendous size alone imbues it with a unique grandeur.

PLATE 34

The field has concentric lozenges of ivory-colored and brown Herati patterns, contained within a dark brown turtle-palmette and flowering vine border, between multiple floral stripes.

Late 19th-Century Tabriz

17' 2" x 12' (5.23 x 3.66 m)

Persia

———⌇———

ONE CAN ONLY WONDER at the skill with which Persian artists have been able to adapt book-binding designs (which, after all, are measured in inches) for use in carpets (which are measured in feet) without loss of charm, balance, or detail.

The underlying aesthetic is essentially an Islamic one. For example, note how the inner segments of each corner are the bases of the arches that support the dome of a mosque. Their presence gives enormous stability to the design as a whole, so that the tracery that encloses the corner can dare to be as fine and as delicate as filigree work.

When viewed from above, as when coming down a wide staircase from an upper floor, the medallion and its appendages float ethereally on a bed of exotic blooms, lovingly held together by a well-defined, traditional border.

PLATE 35

The ivory-colored field has flowering vines around a central, tomato-red cusped medallion with arabesques and medallions and central, indigo, radiating flowerhead, the ivory-colored spandrels with arabesques and flowering vines. It is contained within a tomato-red turtle-palmette and flowering vine border, between triple ivory-colored floral stripes.

Late 19th-Century Tabriz

16' 8" x 11' 5" (5.08 x 3.48 m)

Persia

This great Tabriz carpet reaches heights of perfection that can scarcely be put into words. Its fabulous design and extraordinary workmanship mark it as a carpet of great distinction.

Just look at the intricacy of the design encompassing the central medallion. Like a massive robe of regal office or a view of the heavens seen through a great telescope, this accomplished design makes the heart soar.

Classical, beautiful—this celebrated carpet would be a jewel in any collection.

Plate 36

The ivory-colored field has a concentric brick-red and ivory-colored cusped medallion with floral sprays and arabesques around a central indigo and light blue radiating floral medallion, and the ivory-colored spandrels similar. It is contained within a shaded brick-red border of arabesques and flowering vines, between multiple stripes.

Early 20th-Century Tabriz

15' 6" x 11' (4.72 x 3.35 m)

Persia

THIS IS A VERY HANDSOME decorative carpet, typical of the best work of the early 20th century (note the change in provenance from "Persia" to "Iran.") The carpet boasts a balanced design, harmonious colors, first-class materials, and is extremely well made. Tabriz wools have an enviable reputation—both for their durability and for their readiness to accept, and retain, color.

The designer has outdone himself, using a minimal design repertoire. Note how the alternate, double-headed peacock patterns of the border are repeated in the interstices of the field pattern, and how the nine-leafed palmette pattern is almost identical to the eleven-leafed one in the field.

The interruption in the design at the end of the field is a reminder that, just as we see here only a finite portion of an infinite design, so mankind will only ever understand but a tiny part of the whole of creation. In contrast, meticulous attention has been paid to the border, emphasizing its function as a window frame through which we see Truth. Such insights are privileges, and it would indeed be a privilege to share one's home with such a carpet.

Plate 37

The blood-red field has an overall lattice design with yellow, sand-colored, indigo, and light and medium blue floral palmettes surrounded by minor floral sprays. It is contained within a broad indigo border of large similar palmettes surrounded by flowering vines, between ivory-colored floral stripes.

Late 19th-Century Tabriz

14' 10" x 11' 10" (4.52 x 3.61 m)

PERSIA

———— ⋄ ————

THIS FINE TABRIZ evokes fantasies of the Arabian Nights: marble palaces, colonnaded halls, piled silken cushions enthroning turbaned masters, dancing beauties, jewels, and—of course—the occasional genie!

It is no fantasy to say that this is possibly the most magnificent Tabriz one will ever see. Its classical design simply exudes luxury. To own such a masterpiece would be as rewarding as possessing a fine painting or sculpture—perhaps even more so.

PLATE 38

The shaded turquoise field has palmettes and flowering vines around a shaded brick-red cusped similar medallion with pendants. It is contained within a broad, brick-red turtle-palmette and flowering vine border, between multiple ivory-colored and brick-red floral stripes.

Late 19th-Century Tabriz

14' 8" x 10' 5" (4.47 x 3.18 m)

PERSIA

IT IS NOT DIFFICULT TO SEE why high-quality carpets such as this Tabriz retain their appeal. The muted design and overall coloring make this a carpet ideal for almost any location—classical or modern.

The closer one examines the ground plan of this carpet, the more complex the design reveals itself to be. Based upon geometric precision and strictly formal presentation, the four cut-off corners break the illusion of straight angles in the overall pattern, and the central medallion—again in strictly geometric layout—focuses and holds the attention. The central themes of the composition are formality and perspective, in both of which it is admirably persuasive.

PLATE 39

The pale apricot-hued field has a lattice of floral sprays and lozenges around an ivory-colored Herati medallion, with the spandrels similar. It is contained within an indigo palmette and vine border between multiple floral stripes.

LATE 19TH- CENTURY KIRMAN

14' 5" x 11' 10" (4.39 x 3.61 m)

PERSIA

———— ·◊· ————

IT WOULD BE DIFFICULT to imagine a more assured or refined design than the one displayed in this unusual Kirman.

One's first impression is of a patchwork quilt or a Renaissance cloak. Closer inspection, however, reveals that the design is of numerous individual flowers—some in formal squares, others entwined as if part of a bucolic pagan ritual, such as young girls dancing around the maypole.

Such a carpet inspires imaginative musings. It is a treasure trove of unusual motifs. The carpet's coloring is extremely rare, consisting of unusual subtle monotones. This discreetly beautiful effect adds to its unusual appeal.

PLATE 40

The field has a series of cusped and stepped indigo, ivory-colored, rust-red, and shaded red floral medallions forming concentric lozenge medallions. It is contained within a broad indigo arabesque and flowering vine border, between similar minor stripes.

LATE 19TH-CENTURY BIJAR

14' 2" x 9' 8" (4.32 x 2.95 m)

PERSIA

FIRST IMPRESSIONS can be deceiving. This large carpet from Persia, a Bijar, at first seems full of excessive movement, even violent activity of some kind. On closer examination, however, one realizes that the weaver deliberately created that impression in order to draw attention to the infinitely beautiful pattern "beneath" the surface.

The colorful design, which is framed in a classical border layout, gradually takes on a new significance. This is not the readily understood, uncomplicated design typical of many great Persian carpets but a compelling statement executed with pure artistry.

PLATE 41

The indigo field has a blood-red arabesque lattice enclosing flowerheads and floral sprays. It is contained within a shaded brick-red border of turtle-palmettes and flowering vines, between ivory-colored arabesque and vine stripes.

LATE 19TH-CENTURY KASHAN

14' x 10' (4.27 x 3.05 m)

PERSIA

THIS FABULOUS Kashan carpet owes much of its appeal to the influence of fine jewelry.

The central motifs, for example, may easily be compared with either a necklace or a ring, and the quarter-links framing it could well be the chain upon which it was hung. Jewel-like symbols surround the massive central medallion, and the fiery coloring suggests rubies and yellow diamonds.

The entire carpet glows with a subdued radiance created by harmonious blending of colors.

Such a carpet is rare indeed.

PLATE 42

The shaded tomato-red field has an indigo and ivory-colored cusped and stepped radiating floral medallion, and the spandrels similar. It is contained within a broad indigo palmette and vine border, between multiple ivory-colored and brick-red floral stripes.

Late 19th-Century Tabriz

13' 6" x 10' 6" (4.11 x 3.20 m)

PERSIA

---·◊·---

CONSIDERABLE INGENUITY is on display in the design of this special Tabriz carpet. The centerpiece, with its receding kaleidoscopic effect, is both intriguing and effective. What might otherwise be a plain, uncomplicated decoration becomes a unique, eye-catching design.

The additional motifs, especially in the surrounding borders, add to the total picture without detracting from the clever device used in the center.

Such unique features lift a perfectly ordinary carpet, fine though it might be, out of the mundane into the extraordinary.

PLATE 43

The field has concentric ivory-colored and salmon-pink, Herati-pattern lozenge medallions, contained within a broad rust-red border of turtle-palmettes and flowering vines, between ivory-colored and rust-red floral stripes.

Late 19th-Century Tabriz

13' 4" x 9' 11" (4.06 x 3.02 m)

Persia

Ever since London's Victoria and Albert Museum acquired what was then trumpeted as the most expensive carpet ever, the "Ardebil" has been the most widely known, loved, and copied carpet in the world. These copies naturally vary enormously and, almost invariably, are but a fraction of the size of the originals (there were at least two; one of these—with cannibalized borders—is in the Getty Collection).

Recent research seems to indicate that the carpet was neither made nor found in the city of Ardebil in Persian Azerbaijan. Even so, it must be said that the weavers of Tabriz have long experience in making the most creditable copies of this design. It is greatly to their credit that, unlike many weavers elsewhere, they do not seek to include the cartouche with its famous inscription.

Using the design of a very large carpet to make a copy barely a quarter the size poses considerable problems of adaptation. Many elements must be changed. The most striking difference in design may be found in the treatment of the border, which is now wide enough to make it stand out from the field. This particular border endows the carpet with a three-dimensional appearance. Rather more noticeable is the color palette, which is no longer rich and heavy. In its place, we find soft pastel shades that make this delightful piece immensely light and airy.

Plate 44

The ivory-colored field has palmettes and floral sprays around a large rust-red cusped and radiating medallion with palmettes and cloud band, with radiating pendant medallions, and the spandrels similar. It is contained within a broad rust-red border of palmettes and vines surrounding large, cusped cartouches containing cloud band, between ivory-colored and apricot-hued floral stripes.

Late 19th-Century Tabriz

13' 2" x 10' (4.01 x 3.05 m)

Persia

---·◊·---

THIS TABRIZ CARPET is quite different from what is expected of its genre. In no way does it reflect established notions of Persian carpets as a group. It must, therefore, be assumed that it is unique.

From a design point of view, one is faced with a conundrum: the central panel exhibits a vast array of symbols not readily decipherable, the border motifs are puzzling, and the color palette is very unusual. This is a baffling design—geometric almost to the point of being mathematical, yet intriguing.

Such a masterpiece would shine in a room where it could offset fine furniture and other works of art—an environment where it would be in excellent company.

PLATE 45

The ivory-colored field has staggered rows of alternately facing boteh, *contained within a rust-brown border of ivory-colored flowering vine around large calligraphic cartouches, between multiple floral stripes.*

Late 19th-Century Tabriz

13' 2" x 10' (4.01 x 3.05 m)

PERSIA

REFINED IN BOTH DESIGN AND COLORING, this Tabriz carpet would be completely at home in a classical setting, where it would lend both elegance and charm.

Its highly decorative layout is entirely harmonious. Such a carpet may be viewed time after time and engender only a sense of peace and balance in the onlooker—a gift indeed.

It is the perfect addition to a beautiful setting.

PLATE 46

The pale shaded blue field has staggered rows of stylized cypress trees around a large stepped Herati medallion, and the spandrels similar. It is contained within an ivory-colored palmette and flowering vine border, between light blue and rust-brown floral stripes.

LATE 19TH-CENTURY TABRIZ

13' x 8' 3" (3.96 x 2.51 m)

PERSIA

———·◇·———

THE FORM AND COLOR of the medallion in this carpet is such that, when one views the carpet from a certain height, there is a true 3-D effect, of the kind that has led many rug enthusiasts to believe that the center of the medallion represents "the gates of heaven." Even those who disagree with such views have to admit that this piece is certainly "heavenly!"

Everything about it appears perfect, from the swirling, curling arabesques that wind in and out of the red area (is it the field or is it a large medallion?) to the patterns connecting the palmettes in the border, making them face in alternate directions.

The colors are dark, yet the carpet is light. It is richly patterned, yet the effect is peaceful. The overall impression is one of great dignity; however, such a carpet would be equally at home in a rustic interior. It has outlived the Qajar Dynasty, but seems set to last another hundred years. No wonder dealers regularly complain that "they don't make carpets like this any more."

PLATE 47

The tomato-red field has flowerheads, palmettes, and scrolling arabesques around a large cusped and radiating concentric ivory-colored and indigo medallion with palmettes and flowerheads with vines, and the spandrels similar. It is contained within a broad indigo border of palmettes and vines, between floral stripes.

LATE 19TH-CENTURY TABRIZ

12' 10" x 9' 2" (3.91 x 2.79 m)

PERSIA

———⋄———

LIKE A FIREWORK DISPLAY, or some other celebratory event, this fine Tabriz bursts into life with a fury that ignites the imagination! What other description fits it? How else to describe the magnificent variety of shapes and colors, which seem even more full of activity the more one studies them?

The carpet we see here is totally unlike anything else within the Tabriz range of designs. Nonconformist, avant-garde, and so far in advance of its late 19th-century date it almost denies its own provenance.

Totally unexpected, and in almost every way marvelous, this carpet speaks a language all its own. It will appeal to those adventurous souls with a yen for something completely new in their interiors.

This rare Tabriz is a work of art—comparable with the New Expressionist movement in painting and a powerful adjunct to modern architecture.

PLATE 48

It has an overall lattice of cusped and indented, ivory- and mushroom-colored, fox-brown, light blue, brick-red, sandy-yellow, indigo, and olive-green palmette medallions, surrounded by flowering vines. It is contained within a broad indigo border of floral roundels and sprays, between ivory-colored floral stripes.

Late 19th-Century Tabriz

12' 7" x 9' 7" (3.84 x 2.95 m)

Persia

———·◊·———

EDWARDS, IN HIS MAGISTERIAL BOOK (*The Persian Carpet*, London, 1953), makes clear that the Tabrizi entrepreneurs who reestablished the carpet-weaving industry there at the end of the 19th century unashamedly used the designs of the Kerman carpets of their day. It is, therefore, not surprising that so many early pieces reveal a strong Kermani influence.

In this carpet, the influence is manifest in the border; in the garland of leaves found in each corner; in the trefoil motif that graces the top and the bottom of the field; and in the birds that sit in the trees that cover the field.

The medallion's shape goes back to the times of Shah Abbas. The eight cypress trees that radiate from its center are in the soft muted greens that today are associated with Safavid silks.

Connoisseurs will recognize two other age-old Persian features: the other leaves of the trefoils are based upon the *boteh* design and the equally ubiquitous cloud band has become integrated into the pendants at each end of the medallion. This is subtlety taken to the very edge of genius.

PLATE 49

The ivory-colored field has leafy tendrils and large flower vases around a large, shaded brick-red and ivory-colored radiating floral medallion with pendants. It is contained within an ivory-colored border of flowering vines, between rust-red flowering vine stripes.

Late 19th-Century Tabriz

12' 3" x 10' (3.73 x 3.05 m)

Persia

THIS FINE TABRIZ is noteworthy because it incorporates design motifs seldom seen in a carpet. Among the unusual features are the linked arabesques, which hold together the central motifs and form a unique setting for the floral border.

The high quality and fine execution of this Tabriz marks it as a unique work of art. The colors used are reminiscent of a fine tapestry—a notion enhanced by the floral border, a feature often used in antique tapestries. One is left with an impression of mastery. Such a carpet is deserving of an elegant setting amid complementary furnishings where its beauty can shine.

PLATE 50

The shaded apricot-hued field has an overall lattice of ivory-colored and brown palmettes and floral sprays, contained within an indigo palmette and vine border, between ivory-colored flowering vine and mill-pattern stripes, with plain outer stripe.

Late 19th-Century Tabriz

12'3" x 8'11" (3.73 x 2.72 m)

Persia

———·◇·———

THE IMMEDIATE SURPRISE in this Tabriz is the intricacy of the design. Endless geometric progressions move in seemingly never-ending ramifications. Wherever one's attention moves some new path of exploration opens up.

Even the central medallion itself is set within another, which is also encompassed by a walled garden! Or, perhaps, they are not flowers but a veritable army of warriors? Are the four corners guardian outposts or selected guards overseeing the vast central arena?

A more complex arrangement of motifs would be difficult to imagine, but the visual magnificence of the whole ensemble staggers the mind and commands attention.

Nothing as beautiful comes about by chance and the geometric perfection rules out entirely the notion of an exploratory experiment. The calculated precision of the design has about it the appeal of a mathematical formula, not readily decipherable, but eternally tantalizing.

Plate 51

The indigo field has a Herati pattern in a series of concentric, cusped, and stepped medallions, contained within an ivory-colored flowering vine border, between multiple floral stripes, and plain outer stripe.

Late 19th-Century Tabriz

10' 10" x 8' 8" (3.30 x 2.64 m)

Persia

THE GREAT ADVANTAGE of allover patterns lies in the fact that only a small amount of design, reflected upwards and sideways, needs to be extended to cover a very considerable field. To avoid boredom, however, much skill needs to be exercised in executing such a design. In this carpet we see how well the artist has succeeded in his task: though the basic pattern is about a sixteenth part of the whole, the eye sees the whole.

This effect has been enhanced by the colors that were chosen, and by their maturing over the years to the softer tones we now see.

The use of the much-loved *boteh* design as an overlay of the meander that joins the main motifs adds subtle interest to the border.

The carpet has an air of peace and serenity—qualities eagerly sought in these troubled times.

Plate 52

The ivory-colored field has a counterposed design of radiating floral medallions and floral sprays, contained within a broad indigo border of palmettes and vines, between ivory-colored and brick-red floral stripes.

Late 18th-Century Tabriz

12' 2" x 8' 7" (3.71 x 2.62 m)

Persia

Perhaps the most striking feature of this special Tabriz is the blending of colors. All carpets, of necessity, must have eye appeal, but in this case that appeal includes both color and motif, and the striking juxtaposition of both.

The clever interlocking of the many color variations makes this carpet particularly noteworthy. The design is both sophisticated and enigmatic.

This Tabriz will likely find a home among those buyers with a taste for the exotic. More conventional carpet lovers may find the effect too adventurous, unless they are specifically searching for such a contrast. This carpet is a real attention-getter, with the power to transform the ordinary into the fabulous.

Plate 53

The indigo field has columns of large radiating and indented floral medallions surrounded by arabesques and floral sprays. It is contained within a broad, shaded mid-brown border of large palmettes and flowering vines, between multiple floral stripes.

Early 20th-Century Bezalel

12' x 8' 9" (3.66 x 2.67 m)

Israel

———·◈·———

According to the English poet William Wordsworth, beauty "Dwells in deep retreats" and is often "hidden" by "veils" and disguises. If beauty is in the eye of the beholder, fashion and taste serve as—albeit temporary—arbiters in the matter.

This is particularly true when it comes to fine carpets. Although style and fashion dictate most decisions, quality—both of design and manufacture—is never out of date. Fine art, whether it be a painting, a sculpture, or a carpet, speaks with a universal language.

This fine Israeli carpet blends form, design, color, imagery, and craftsmanship, thereby creating a very harmonious work of art. The Birds of Paradise and Trees of Life are all beautifully incorporated into their Garden of Eden and framed in a setting of rare beauty.

Plate 54

The shaded brick-red field has large, stylized flowering trees surrounded by flowering plants and a variety of bird. It is contained within a broad, pale blue border of palmettes, flowering vines, and animal combat groups, between ivory-colored and light blue palmettes and flowering vine stripes.

Late 19th-Century Tabriz

12' x 8' 9" (3.66 x 2.67 m)

Persia

———— ·◊· ————

Many of the early looms used by carpet weavers in Tabriz were constructed of timbers that were to weak to withstand the weight they had to support and the tensions imposed by the stringing of the warps. The prohibitive cost of upgrading the looms meant that many of the earlier Tabriz pieces failed to achieve rectangular perfection, once they were cut down from the loom and placed on the floor. In a modern rug, such imperfections would be anathema, yet in an antique carpet are perfectly acceptable—and even contribute to the carpet's charm.

By the time this rug was woven, Tabriz weavers had established a repertoire of designs and color preferences that are readily seen here. This Tabriz carpet displays fine draftsmanship, dyeing, and weaving—all hallmarks of a fine carpet. Of note, too, is the strong evidence of curvilinear designs so often seen in Tabriz carpets. These peculiar elements have a feminine sensibility, yet the overall effect is robust and masculine.

Plate 55

The ivory-colored field has a concentric fox-brown and ivory-colored cusped and scalloped medallion, containing palmettes and floral sprays with a central indigo floral medallion, and the spandrels similar. It is contained within a rust-red palmette and vine border, between multiple floral stripes.

Late 19th-Century Bijar

11' 8" x 6' 7" (3.56 x 2.01 m)

PERSIA

———·◇·———

Perhaps the most startling thing about human creativity is its inventiveness.

This magnificent Persian carpet from Bijar is an excellent example. Few carpets create such a powerful first impression. The meaning of the carpet is not readily apparent, but the daring design intrigues right away.

On closer examination, one notices that the four corners incorporate an unusually large variety of florets. The rectangular centerpiece benefits from heightened colors and design and provides a sharp contrast with the overall design.

Whatever its esoteric "message," this carpet conveys a more readily understood message of power and confidence. At the same time, the profusion of flowers softens the dominant overtones.

Plate 56

The ivory-colored field has columns of cypress trees and floral matrices, with branches with serrated leaves around a large, shaded brick-red Herati-pattern medallion with large, blue, hooked floral pendants, the indigo spandrels with Herati pattern. It is contained within a narrow, pale blue, flowering vine border, between mill-pattern stripes, a brick-red panel of turtle-palmettes, and with flowering vines at each end.

Early 20th-Century Indian

18' x 11' 8" (5.49 x 3.56 m)

India

THE 19TH CENTURY saw the beginning of a social revolution in England and the introduction for the first time of a "middle-class." Much of England's new wealth came from the creation of the middle class and, as a result, the market for art and furnishings saw enormous growth.

This very special Indian carpet displays a richness of design and color largely influenced by Mogul traditions. The whirl of sabers, the interplay of intense sunlight on sandstone villages, and the magnificence of that vast subcontinent all seem to be reflected in the repetitive design of this carpet. The linked arabesques are a motif particularly associated with India. Any Persian influences observable only add to the magical qualities of the carpet, which benefits from the long artistic traditions of both cultures.

PLATE 57

The shaded rust-red field has a pale yellow and salmon-pink lattice enclosing a variety of floral sprays, some against an indigo background. It is contained within a pale yellow border of curling flowering vines, between multiple floral stripes.

LATE 19TH-CENTURY AGRA

17' 6" x 14' 2" (5.33 x 4.32 m)

INDIA

THE EXTRAORDINARY THING about this massive Agra carpet is the startling juxtaposition of the symbols used. The lightning-like creeper entwined throughout the border is spellbinding and very unusual.

As one looks more closely, however, several underlying motifs begin to reveal themselves: a maze of endless duration, cathedral-like windows, flowers, and stars. These features ensure that this is a carpet that one can look at again and again and always see new elements.

The only appropriate word for this carpet is vital. Few carpets have this impact, but this Agra does so and more.

PLATE 58

The ivory-colored field has golden angular vines with floral tendrils around a massive, shaded wine-red, cusped and indented palmette and flowering vine medallion. It is contained within a shaded wine-red border of palmettes, flowering vines, and arabesques, between floral and plain stripes.

Late 19th-Century Amritzar

16' 8" x 14' (5.08 x 4.27 m)

India

THE SIZE AND COLOR of this Amritzar carpet are its most appealing features.

The leaves and florets appear to be autumnal, and the carpet as a whole uses a number of earth tones that might preclude certain furnishing schemes but complement others.

A study or library might offer the perfect setting for such a sophisticated carpet, where the very softness of the visual impact could harmonize with the atmosphere of contemplation and study.

On the other hand, a very bright location could well enhance the colors of the carpet and provide a contrast to more vibrant colors in the room—such as yellow and green.

Plate 59

The pale shaded lilac field has columns of dark brown palmettes and medallions surrounded by serrated leaves and flowering vines. It is contained within a mid-brown palmette and angular vine border, between flowering vines and mill-pattern stripes.

Late 19th-Century Indian

16' 9" x 16' (5.11 x 4.88 m)

India

———⋅◇⋅———

MANY BUYERS FIND IT DIFFICULT to distinguish the best Indian carpets of the late 19th century from their Persian contemporaries. One giveaway is that Indian weavers were more careful in selecting materials and dyeing them than their Persian counterparts, so that the finished product is always better finished. As a result, Indian carpets suffer less from the *abradj* so common in Persian goods.

This is evident in this handsome square carpet, which displays mainly pastel-toned patterns gracefully integrated on a cream-colored field. It has symmetry yet is never boring. There is just enough dark blue to give strength to the overall design and to enable the borders to properly contain the field.

PLATE 60

The pale yellow field has an overall design of palmettes and flowering vines with leafy tendrils and indigo spandrels with arabesques and floral motifs. It is contained within an ivory-colored turtle-palmette and flowering vine border, between flowering vines and plain stripes.

LATE 19TH-CENTURY AGRA

16' 2" x 12' 11" (4.93 x 3.94 m)

INDIA

———⊙———

THE RICH DESIGN of this extraordinary carpet is greatly enhanced by the rare, luminous red of the field. It is a quality found only in the very best Indian carpets.

The design appears to be derived from an early palace carpet—the kind that is long and narrow, with a single, extended medallion with corners. Since there are two equally important medallions side by side, one infers that this piece was designed for an audience chamber, where two equally powerful rulers would sit together.

The feeling of majesty and power that this charismatic piece so proudly proclaims is boosted by the intricacy of the supporting designs. To the uninitiated, the political subtext found within the Shah Abbas motifs may be less obvious. Instead of being boldly drawn and connected with equally bold arabesques, the flowers and leaves that cover the field are depicted on a small scale and are connected in an insignificant manner.

From the way the designer has incorporated these motifs, it would have been clear to any educated Indian or Persian of the day that the power of British India was considered superior to that of Persia. Such reflections of superiority were not restricted to India; for their part, the Safavid shahs of Persia would present foreigners with gifts of fine silken textiles that had been patterned in such a way as to communicate the perceived superiority of the Persian monarchs.

This prestigious carpet was undoubtedly created at the peak of Britain's imperial power for the use and pleasure of the viceroy and vicereine of India.

PLATE 61

The dark wine-red field has an overall design of massive, cusped, gray-and-steel-blue, concentric medallions surrounded by arabesques and palmettes and flowering vines. It is contained within a narrow ivory-colored border of flowering vines between mill-pattern and flowering vine stripes.

LATE 19TH-CENTURY AGRA

16' x 9' 10" (4.88 x 3 m)

INDIA

———·◊·———

A WONDERFULLY DECORATIVE REWORKING of the design of an early 16th-century masterpiece, formerly in the Robinson Collection[1], then in the Yerkes Collection[2], and currently a prized possession of the Metropolitan Museum of Art in New York[3].

The principal motif in the field is a curvilinear, eight-sided figure, which, were it rectilinear (as Mumford points out in his commentary on the Yerkes carpet), would be the star of divinity.

With the exception of unidirectional designs, the focal point of a carpet is its center. In this carpet, the positioning of the darker patterns takes the eye away from the central motif, with the result that the focus actually lies in the center of the lefthand border. It is as if the carpet were intended to be placed sideways against a stage, and that it was necessary for all eyes to converge on the person in the middle of that stage.

This train of thought leads one to conclude that this carpet may have been created for the public room of a palace, for use by a very high-ranking personage, if not the rajah himself.

1. Robinson (Vincent J.). *Eastern Carpets. Twelve Early Examples.* London, 1882. Plate 3
2. Mumford. *The Yerkes Collection.* New York, 1910. Plate XXV
3. Dimand and Mailey. *Oriental Rugs in the Metropolitan Museum.* New York, 1973. Catalog No. 6 (color plate I, b&w plate 67).

PLATE 62

The ivory-colored field has an overall design of off-white, pale sand, and shaded wine-red, cusped cartouches and roundels, containing a wide variety of stylized floral motifs and animal combat groups. It is contained within a broad ivory-colored border, with wine-red cartouches containing cloud band and tracery vines surrounded by flowering vines, in a broad sand-colored border of tracery vines and flowerheads.

Late 19th-Century Amritzar

15' 6" x 10' 9" (4.72 x 3.28 m)

India

———⋄———

When British power in India was at its height, the officers' quarters in Poona, Rawalpindi, and other outposts of the British Empire would have been furnished with pieces similar to this Amritzar carpet. One can easily imagine a pale-faced, young subaltern, fresh from Britain, getting a dressing down by his colonel, or, to use the vernacular, "being carpeted," on just such a masculine-looking rug.

Everything about the design speaks of authority, discipline, and reliability. There isn't a pattern or knot out of place. Handsome and exceptionally well woven, a century later this fine carpet still carries itself with pride and dignity.

Plate 63

The pale yellow field has staggered rows of palmette lozenge medallions, contained within a brick-red border of flowering plants between multiple, flowering vine stripes, and plain outer stripe.

LATE 19TH-CENTURY AMRITZAR

15' 4" x 11' 4" (4.67 x 3.45 m)

INDIA

IF EVER A CARPET embodied the splendor of its origins, this great Amritzar certainly does.

The colors alone bring to mind fantasies of Mogul splendor. The centerpiece blazes like an imperial jewel, and the richly decorated setting expresses the magnificence of important surroundings.

This Indian carpet proudly exhibits national pride. Whatever the meaning of the hieroglyphics decorating the borders, self-effacement can certainly be ruled out.

PLATE 64

The ivory-colored field has a cloud band, flowering vines, and animals around a large, shaded wine-red, scalloped palmette and vine medallion. The broad ivory-colored border has a cloud band and flowering vine around large, shaded steel-blue calligraphic and floral cartouches, divided by wine-red, scalloped, floral roundels.

LATE 19TH-CENTURY AGRA

14' 9" x 12' 6" (4.50 x 3.81 m)

INDIA

THE INTERNATIONAL REPUTATION of Agra carpets is enhanced by fine specimens such as this. It vibrates with so many classical overtones that one could be excused for thinking it must have come from another era and another country. Its similarity to carpets from Persia is a compliment, but, almost a hundred years old, it echoes an allegiance only, for it is Indian and a great tribute to its makers.

There are many romantic associations here, not least of which is the imperial grandeur expressed in the colors chosen. This is a rug that would not be out of place on the marble floor of a fine palace, in the midst of untold wealth, and trodden upon by dreamy-eyed women in beautiful saris.

PLATE 65

The shaded brick-red field has an overall lattice design of palmettes, flowerheads, and floral sprays. It is contained within a broad indigo palmette and flowering vine border, between multiple ivory-colored and red flowerheads and flowering vine stripes.

LATE 19TH-CENTURY AMRITZAR

14' 7" x 9' 10" (4.44 x 3 m)

INDIA

IT IS A TRADITION in both book binding and architecture to employ inscriptions as a major design element. Since these two art forms were the main sources of carpet design in the time of Shah Abbas, it is hardly surprising that one finds carpets that also include inscriptions

The beauty of the inscriptions was never in question, for, in the past, the quotations were taken from the Holy Koran. Quotations of a more private nature were taken from Hafiz, Sa'adi, and other great Persian poets. The field of such a carpet was often taken to be a microcosm of the natural world, which is why animals abound. Design concepts of this nature have been around for many centuries.

The creator of this fine Amritzar has dipped into both these traditions and come up with a jewel-like design. The many-lobed medallion is perhaps the most surprising element of the design because it is so unusual. It sits proudly on a field covered with all manner of beasts. Even the cloud band motif along the vertical axis has become a serpent.

This would have been a very tense and busy carpet in traditional colors, so it is fortunate that, in this instance, tradition was ignored. Instead, an ivory-colored field, a silvery medallion, much light blue, and only a modicum of red have been used, leaving us with a feeling of peace and relaxation.

PLATE 66

The ivory-colored field has palmettes, vines, and a cloud band surrounding a variety of animals, with a central, ivory-colored, scalloped medallion with arabesques and tracery vines. It is contained within a broad, ivory-colored border of palmettes and vines, surrounding shaded dark aubergine-colored calligraphic and floral cartouches divided by light blue roundels, between ivory-colored and light blue floral stripes.

Late 19th-Century Amritzar

13' 4" x 10' (4.06 x 3.05 m)

India

Heraldic symbols are more common in tapestries than in carpets. In this instance, though, the motif used is reminiscent of a crusader's tunic or a French emblem of nobility, albeit decorative. Nevertheless, the entire carpet is dominated by this amazing cartouche. The form and color all indicate a special heraldic purpose, but none is apparent. The carpet as a whole—set within a formal border—is very compelling and succeeds extremely well.

This unusual carpet would be a tremendous asset to any room.

Plate 67

The shaded blue field has ivory-colored tracery floral vines around a large, tomato-red, cusped medallion containing palmettes and flowering vines around a large ivory-colored palmette and tracery vine medallion with pendants, with similar ivory-colored spandrels. It is contained within an ivory-colored palmette and arabesque vine border, between multiple, shaded blue and ivory-colored floral stripes.

Late 19th-Century Amritzar

12' 8" x 10' (3.86 x 3.05 m)

India

THIS IS A CARPET that can truly be said to have flair. Decorated with massive floral patterns, the design as a whole is nevertheless controlled and organized.

It lacks esoteric motifs and a subliminal "message." This lively Amritzar promises nothing more than to be a handsome addition to a splendid room—the purpose for which it was designed. It succeeds on all counts.

Plate 68

The shaded wine-red field has an overall lattice of apricot-hued and steel-blue palmette medallions and arabesques. It is contained within a broad aubergine-colored border of flowering vines surrounding floral cartouches and medallions, between ivory-colored palmettes, arabesque vines, and angular stripes.

Late 19th-Century Amritzar

12' x 9' (3.66 x 2.74 m)

India

Enclosed within a zig-zag border, with crosses in the outer triangles, this carpet displays a truly remarkable amount of meticulously woven detail, warmly rendered in border and field alike, in delightfully pale colors. There is no medallion, but the carpet has a very clear focal point.

Most of the minor patterns are derived from the Shah Abbas school of designs, albeit interpreted in a typically Indian manner.

The color scheme is utterly charming, and would be an asset in almost any interior.

Plate 69

The ivory-colored field has an overall lattice design of indigo and brick-red palmettes and flowering vines, contained within a broad ivory-colored border of angular lozenge medallions, surrounded by feathery leaves and angular vines, between reciprocal stepped, mill-pattern, and flowering vine stripes.

LATE 19TH-CENTURY AGRA

11'11" x 9' (3.63 x 2.74 m)

INDIA

SOMETIMES IT IS NOT EASY to separate the ordinary from the unusual, since taste and fashion exert their separate influences.

This happens when a carpet falls into neither category. On the one hand, it conforms to the established strictures; on the other, it follows a trend of its own.

This Agra carpet is a case in point. Until one looks closely, it does not appear to be particularly different from many others. A more thorough examination, however, reveals that the carpet has many unique features. One unusual aspect is the colors that have been used. It is rare to use two-fold coloring, especially cream and brown. The center panel repeats the color duo, thereby ensuring that no individual motif is given a color distinction. The whole effect is one of clarity and formality. In this respect, the carpet is both classical and individual.

PLATE 70

The ivory-colored field has an overall lattice of wine-red palmettes, flowering vines, and cypress trees, contained within a broad, wine-red border of palmettes and flowering vines, between multiple, brown, flowering vines and S-pattern stripes.

Mid-19th-Century Agra

11' 10" x 11' 10" (3.61 x 3.61 m)

India

Those familiar with the great country houses of England will recollect having seen strapwork in all manner of places (the most striking examples of which are richly worked plaster ceilings). Strapwork is, of course, frequently found in embroidery and needlework, some of which was certainly used to decorate the frames of pictures and mirrors. This is why the bold strapwork design of this carpet's border, whose corners are such that they could easily have featured a family's coat of arms, has such a European flavor.

This leads one to wonder whether the designer who was commissioned to make this carpet, using this particular Persian or Mughal miniature, was so impressed by the sophistication of the framing that he decided to use the former as inspiration for the field, and the latter as inspiration for the border. He has successfully married the two by the deceptively simple technique of having the colors of the field infiltrate the designs of the border.

As for the patterning of the field, this is a wonderfully symbolic and meticulously executed representation of the jungle. Birds observe jackals lying in wait for marauding lions, which in turn, bring down fleeing deer. The whole drama hardly touches the elephant, who continues his peaceful meal seemingly oblivious to what is going on around him.

Taken as a whole, the carpet is marvelously balanced. The border's inner guard emphasizes the merits of symmetry. The rich deep tones harmonize with each other, with the reddish hues of the field lightening the dark blue of the border, yet somehow conspiring to give the whole a mysterious golden aura.

Anyone who has dedicated many years to the study and appreciation of Oriental rugs will know that exciting finds like this carpet are all too rare, and that one must often wait a lifetime to discover such a fine specimen. This Agra makes the heart race with the excitement of discovery and thrills us with its mastery.

Plate 71

The shaded wine-red field has a central column of cypress and flowering trees, surrounded by a multitude of animals and birds, including elephants, lions, deer, rabbits, and wolves set among a wide variety of flowering trees, floral sprays, and floral palmettes. It is contained within a broad, indigo border of blood-red, cusped, tracery vines enclosing, and surrounded by, floral sprays and palmettes, between pale yellow, flowering vine stripes.

Late 19th-Century Amritzar

11' 10" x 8' (3.61 x 2.44 m)

India

NOT A SINGLE MOTIF in this exuberant design can be called subservient to the whole. The entire carpet seems to struggle for one's attention.

Smoldering beneath the volcanic coloring, the various motifs battle for prominence—like some stage in the evolution of life itself.

The symbols are mystical. It is hard to say whether they represent anything within the known world. Set within very formal borders, the central cartouche grips the imagination and leads one to speculate about its meaning.

This important Amritzar carpet is baffling, yet it offers the viewer spectacle and fascination. Few carpets ever do both.

Plate 72

The shaded blue and aubergine-colored field has a central column of large palmettes and arabesques surrounded by flowering vines. It is contained within a broad, wine-red border of angular flowerheads and vines, between double flowering vine stripes, with plain, outer, steel-blue stripe.

Late 19th-Century Amritzar

11' 9" x 8' 10" (3.58 x 2.69 m)

India

As POPULATIONS become more advanced, they usually feel the need to break away entirely from former modes of expression.

On the whole, Amritzar carpets are usually less sober than this example, which indicates a new, restrained, even formal style. Fortunately, the Mogul tradition is still very much in evidence. The curves and colors are clearly influenced by that era. It doesn't take much to imagine the gentle sway of dancing maidens, the soft silk of a bejewelled turban, and, in the distance, the strange sounds of sitar music.

A carpet such as this offers as good a reason as any to celebrate the rich cultural traditions of the world—to glory in our differences, as well as our similarities.

Plate 73

The plain, shaded golden field has a massive, central, wine-red, cusped palmette and flowerhead medallion, and spandrels with palmettes and flowering vines. It is contained within a broad, wine-red border of flowerheads and arabesque vines, between ivory-colored and shaded golden flowering vines and mill-pattern stripes, and plain outer stripe.

Late 19th-Century Amritzar

11' 8" x 10' 2" (3.56 x 3.10 m)

India

Not everyone wants—or needs—a carpet that "makes a statement." On many occasions, all that is required is for the carpet to be a beautiful, softly colored counterpoint to the furniture that rests upon it or the people who walk over it.

Here is a wonderfully neutral piece, whose spacious design could as easily have been inspired by the Orient as by the courts of Europe. The understated colors confirm as much.

For all its delicacy, this is nevertheless a well-made and sturdy carpet that, given the right surroundings, should make the perfect houseguest.

Plate 74

The pale sand-colored field has a counterposed design of palmettes and floral spray, contained within a border of floral sprays and cartouches, between serrated and floral stripes.

Late 19th-Century Amritzar

11' x 9' (3.35 x 2.74 m)

India

IN A LAND WHERE THE SUN is often so bright that everything else fades into insignificance, it is not surprising to find this golden-toned carpet from Amritzar. The classical symbols—especially the mosque domes joined in the central medallion—offer an whole effect that is limpid and beautiful.

Where other carpets express nationalistic symbols—beautiful as they are—this Amritzar celebrates sunlight.

Such sensitivity is not always apparent in Indian carpets—reflecting, as they often do, outside influences, especially from Persia; yet, this Amritzar reveals a unique Indian characteristic: gentility with overtones of quiet confidence.

Plate 75

The plain ivory-colored field has a large, central, pale yellow, cusped floral medallion, issuing floral sprays, the spandrels with part palmette medallions. It is contained within a broad ivory-colored border of aubergine-colored palmette cartouches surrounded by flowering vines, between ivory-colored flowering vines and plain aubergine-colored stripes, and plain outer ivory-colored stripe.

Late 19th-Century Amritzar

11' x 10' (3.35 x 3.05 m)

India

THIS IS A CARPET WHOSE DESIGN has been heavily influenced by jewelry, and its elements are most easily described in that vein. The medallion is like a many-faceted jewel in an ornate mount with four equally ornate clasps springing from it. Like jewelry laid out on a rich, flowered brocade, these elements are displayed on a densely patterned floral field. Even the border is reminiscent of a sterling silver photograph frame.

This analogy does not hold true when one considers the colors used in this piece. Instead of employing a brilliant garnet red, a hue that would have been powerful beyond words, the weavers used soft, muted colors. The carpet is dignified and well mannered, and its design is hugely successful.

Interestingly, the PreRaphaelite Brotherhood, led by William Morris and his peers along with several disciples, claimed that much of their work was inspired by the designs of the East. This carpet does seem to back up their claim, for one can easily imagine it as the inspiration for 19th-century English artists. Naturally, one cannot compare the efforts of English weavers—no matter how talented—with those of Indian or Persian weavers, who were born into the world of carpet weaving. To confuse the two is like comparing an expensive meal in a smart, air-conditioned "French" restaurant in Manhattan with a cheap repast enjoyed under the vines on the terrace of a small country hotel in the heart of France.

PLATE 76

The shaded steel-blue field has a large cusped floral medallion surrounded by large beige and tomato-red palmettes and arabesques and flowering vines. It is contained within a broad sandy-yellow border of angular, stylized, flowering vines and palmettes, between ivory-colored palmettes and flowering vine stripes, and plain outer shaded steel-blue stripe.

Late 19th-Century Amritzar

10' 5" x 9' 6" (3.18 x 2.90 m)

India

---·◇·---

This Amritzar carpet, with its original symbols and fascinating calligraphy, immediately spins romantic fantasies.

The symbols can only be translated with the help of someone who speaks Arabic or Urdu. Even so, one can easily imagine that they might have religious implications or be poetic.

In this carpet, one sees heaven and earth represented by stars and flowers. The four corners of the earth look upon the heavens in adulation, while birds of paradise guard the Garden of Eden.

This almost square rug is a thing of great beauty, no matter how we interpret its story.

Plate 77

The caramel field has a cloud band, arabesques, and flowering vines around a large central medallion with peacocks and a cloud band surrounded by ivory-colored and pale rose-colored floral cartouches. It is contained within a broad apricot-hued border of dark wine-red cartouches containing pale rose-colored, flowering, tracery vines around calligraphic inscriptions, divided by pale olive-colored floral medallions and surrounded by a stylized cloud band, between ivory-colored and pale rust-colored, angular, flowering vine stripes.

LATE 19TH CENTURY AGRA

9' x 7' 6" (2.74 x 2.29 m)

INDIA

———·◈·———

THE DESIGN OF THIS AGRA CARPET offers a feast for the imagination.

Here, we enter a fairyland where nothing is real or recognizable. Floating clouds, entangled flowers, and tiny lights flicker in what looks to be an autumnal landscape.

The colors used are vibrant and rich, yet the symbols appear to have no meaning. One cannot say for sure whether the weaver intended some of his motifs to be leaves, flowers, or other natural elements. Ultimately, it is all left to our imagination.

This Agra speaks to us softly in dulcet tones, and we are drawn to its magic.

PLATE 78

The shaded rust-colored field has an overall design of large ivory-colored palmettes and pale yellow leaves surrounded by smaller leaves and flowers. It is contained within a broad, pale turquoise-hued palmette and vine border, between mill-pattern stripes and a plain brick-red outer stripe.

Late 19th-Century Borlu

15' 2" x 11' 5" (4.62 x 3.48 m)

Turkey

This restrained Borlu breathes sophistication and projects quiet dignity and self-confidence. Its pedigree comes through in every fiber.

The ease with which the individual motifs harmonize in the design says a great deal about the skill of the weaver. The colors chosen are easy on the eye and calm the senses.

It is a carpet that should be used to set a certain mood in a room, not merely as decoration.

Plate 79

The ivory-colored field has a tracery design of palmettes, floral lozenges, flowering vines, and leafy sprays around a central, open, floral medallion. It is contained within a palmette and flowering vine border, between multiple floral and reciprocal stripes.

LATE 19TH-CENTURY BORLU

13' 2" x 8' 6" (4.01 x 2.59 m)

TURKEY

THE MOST IMPORTANT STYLISTIC FEATURE of this carpet is its limpid coloring. This clever ploy provokes interest and examination—much like the veil that hides a beautiful face entices the onlooker.

The extraordinary thing is that the more one looks, the more discoveries one makes. Clever arabesques link arms with what appear to be chandeliers, while the intriguing border is satisfyingly classical.

Many of the features in this fascinating design are overplayed in less subtle carpets. Although variations on its themes abound, the lyrical setting of this particular carpet is rare and extremely beautiful.

PLATE 80

The shaded rose-colored field has two columns of stylized cypress trees and floral cartouches with palmettes and floral sprays. It is contained within a broad ivory-colored border of palmettes and angular, stylized cypress trees, between pale golden, reciprocal and flowering vine stripes, and a plain outer stripe.

Late 19th-Century Sparta

12' 10" x 10' (3.91 x 3.05 m)

Turkey

———⋅∾⋅———

THE CAREFUL GEOMETRY of this carpet from Sparta seems to belie its origin, for Turkish people give the impression of being fiery in temperament and given to excitement. Yet, here, in this magnificent Sparta rug, we have an order and symmetry so precise it could be the ground plan for a series of formal gardens.

The formality extends to the myriad esoteric symbols. Even the flowers growing in the pots seem balanced on geometric pivots. And the attention-getting centerpiece defies explanation. Maybe it represents the Hanging Gardens of Babylon, with eddying waters moving in opposing directions in a river?

Whatever the meaning (and one longs to know!), the overall effect is one of grandeur and handsomeness.

Plate 81

The field has a garden design, comprising stylized waterways with fish forming a cruciform and a central pond surrounded by areas of stylized plants and flowerheads. It is contained within a reciprocal border of fleurs-de-lys, between ivory-colored flowerhead stripes and plain outer stripe.

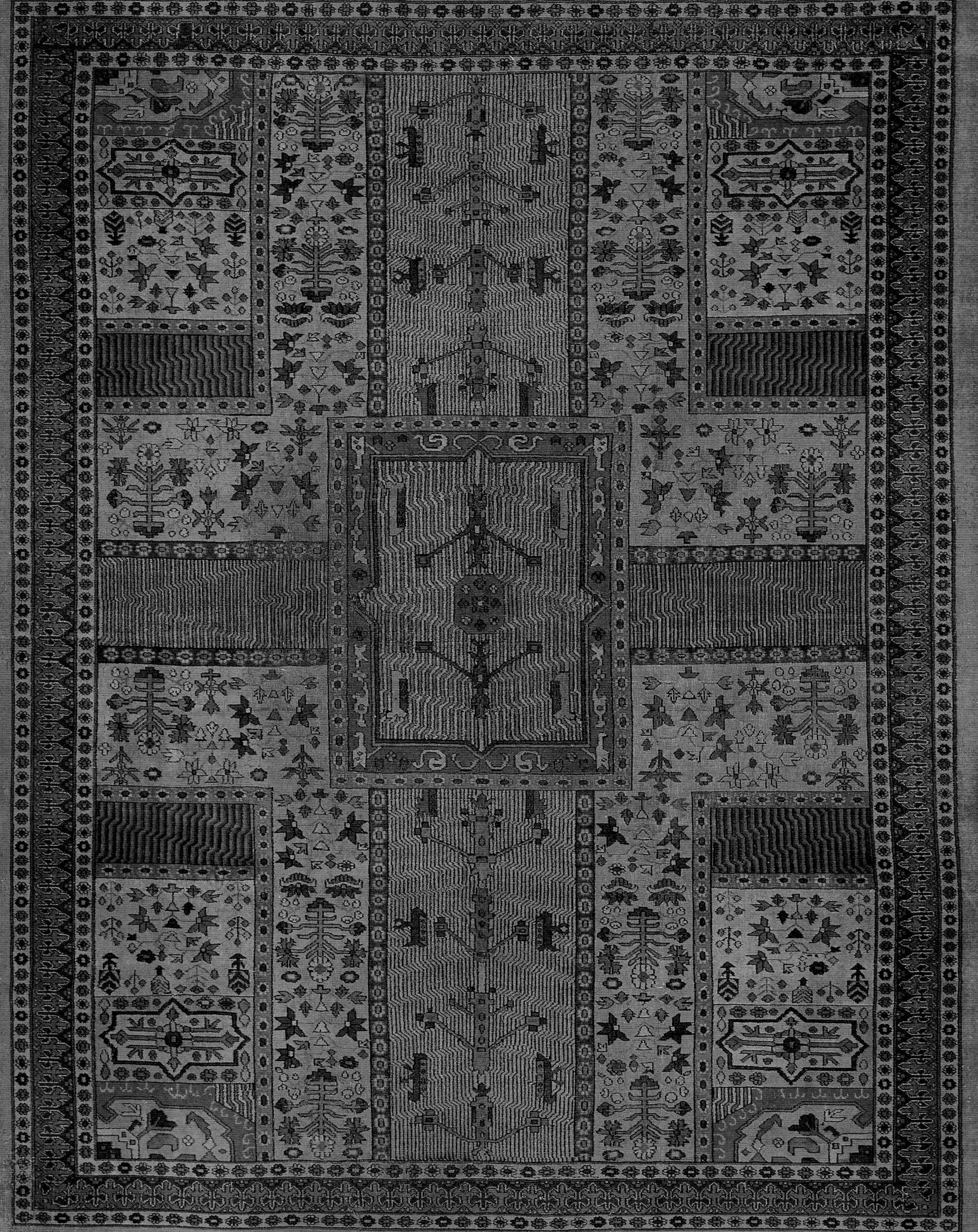

LATE 19TH-CENTURY SIVAS

12' 3" x 9' 7" (3.73 x 2.92 m)

TURKEY

THIS UNUSUAL SIVAS is destined to play a starring role in the decor of a fine room. Its dominant design and colors may even lead it to serve as the central theme for an entire room.

The format is rare. The basic geometry, while somewhat eccentric, is carefully contained within strictly formal boundaries. Any chance of eclecticism is reined in within a readily comprehensible border, containing flowers, ribbons, and stars. This wonderful contrast is just one reason why this carpet would be a handsome addition to any setting.

PLATE 82

The ivory-colored field has a multitude of flowering tendrils and sprays around a large tomato-colored lozenge medallion with weeping willows and floral matrices in an indigo similar frame. It is contained within an indigo border of ivory-colored floral roundels and tomato-colored, floral tendrils surrounded by flowering vines, between multiple floral stripes.

LATE 19TH-CENTURY OUSHAK

12' x 9' (3.66 x 2.74 m)

TURKEY

———·◊·———

IN THE LATE 19TH-CENTURY, nothing except for the size would have been recognizable in this very special Oushak carpet from Turkey.

In England, especially, 12 feet by 9 feet was almost a universal size for a carpet, although the color and design of this particular rug would not typically have been to English taste. For that, one can thank the Arts and Crafts movement, which caused the intelligentsia to think again.

Architects Frank Lloyd Wright and Edward Lutyens and designer William Morris threw off their cloaks of conformity and, in a frenzy of experimentation, moved England and America into the 20th century. Early 20th-century movements such as Art Nouveau and Art Deco suddenly made the world seem a new and exciting place. It had the effect of blowing away the cobwebs of the old century.

Minor masterpieces such as this Oushak were not only part of the process but in the vanguard. It has the honor of being one of a very few carpets that were created during that unusual time period.

PLATE 83

The golden field has a stylized lattice of indigo, tomato-colored, and light blue palmettes and tendrils surrounded by flowering tendrils. It is contained within a tomato-colored border of palmettes and vines, between apricot-hued and light blue lozenges and stylized, angular vine stripes.

Late 19th-Century Samarkand

10' 5" x 7' (3.18 x 2.13 m)

Russia

———·◇·———

THERE ARE MANY LEGENDS about Samarkand. One such legend claims that certain roads lead there! But what would one find at the end of one's journey? Strange buildings much like mud-igloos in the native quarters; dusty streets filled with traders and soothsayers; and, of course, palaces and great buildings.

Somewhere, amid the clamor of commerce and the throng of people, would be the carpet makers. Renowned throughout history, they sit cross-legged plying their trade at looms that rattle in the heat of the sun. The pace of life is slow here—and the carpets are as magical as ever.

In this particular carpet, for example, we see a forest of symbols—all linked in rows, like sentinels guarding a courtyard festooned with banners and trophies. The effect is fabulous in the extreme.

PLATE 84

The shaded indigo field has two columns of stylized, flowering pomegranate trees, contained within a multiple-striped border of panels of stylized flowerheads and a mill pattern.

LATE 19TH-CENTURY KARABAGH

9' x 3' 10" (2.74 x 1.17 m)

UKRAINE

KARABAGH—even the name evokes mystery and romance. Who knows its meaning, but one can at least get an idea when one looks at this long carpet. Exciting, certainly not placid, contemptuous, in fact, of all formality, this Karabagh carpet strikes a lively chord. Enhanced by floral displays, it moves along with a thrilling momentum, unchecked even by its flimsy border.

It has about it more than a suggestion of the art of the tapestry. It might make an attractive wall hanging even, although it is clearly intended as a carpet runner. No matter where it is placed, the masterly hand that worked this design made sure it would never be overlooked.

PLATE 85

The indigo field has a mass of stylized flower-heads and floral sprays around large shaded golden curling acanthus, contained within ivory-colored tracery vines, in a mill-pattern border.

LATE 19TH-CENTURY KARABAGH

8' 10" x 7' 2" (2.69 x 2.18 m)

UKRAINE

———— ·◇· ————

THIS MAGNIFICENT KARABAGH carpet leaves one almost speechless with its beauty.

It has the effect that stained-glass windows in a great cathedral might have, of literally taking one's breath away. It is not so much the subject matter that causes this effect, but the combination of color and grandeur, which together are sufficient to engender awe and amazement.

So it is that we can set aside any attempts to interpret the symbolism of this carpet and concentrate instead on its beauty. This is a masterpiece on the scale of, say, a Braque or a Picasso.

Expressionism was in its infancy when this carpet was created, and one is tempted to speculate that it might be a forerunner to the late great works found in that movement.

Ultimately, all that really matters is that this carpet is a thing of beauty that enchants each time one looks at it.

PLATE 86

The indigo field has golden, curling stylized vines with large palmettes and floral sprays, contained within a broad similar border, between mill-pattern stripes.

Late 19th-Century Bessarabian

9' x 6' (2.74 x 1.83 m)

Ukraine

THE PROVENANCE of this unusual Bessarabian carpet will not be immediately apparent to many people.

In fact, one could be excused for thinking that is a tapestry, not a carpet at all. The overall visual effect is of fine workmanship and a somewhat childlike design, more often associated with peasant craftwork.

Since it is from the Ukraine—a vast and endlessly fascinating area—this may very well be the case. There is a joyful simplicity to the piece, coupled with a quality of execution that makes one want to hang it on a wall rather than tread on it.

The rug displays a naivete that is altogether charming.

Plate 87

The shaded ivory-colored field has large indigo and shaded raspberry-colored flowerheads and vines around a large open olive-green floral medallion, contained within a broad blue border of flowering vines.

LATE 19TH-CENTURY SAVONNERIE

20' x 17' 8" (6.10 x 5.38 m)

SPAIN

ONE LOOK AT THIS FABULOUS CARPET and the magic of Old Spain immediately springs to mind. The whirl of flamenco dancers, the rhythm of stamping feet, the sun-drenched colors, and the clamor and dust of the bullring seem to erupt from this brilliantly executed design.

Exotic in the extreme, triumphal wreaths, Moorish crescent moons, even the dome of the Alhambra and the arcades of Aranjuez seem somehow to be woven into the very fabric and colors of the pattern. All that is missing is the romantic strumming of a hundred guitars.

There is nothing in this entire catalog to remotely compare with this very Spanish work of art. What the Aubusson is to France, this carpet is to Spain.

PLATE 88

The steel-gray field has tan and ivory-colored, plain, curling, and serrated leaves around a similar roundel with gray and light blue acanthus with a central yellow floral roundel centerpiece. It is contained within a similar border with rose-colored batons, between plain stripes.

Early 20th-Century Savonnerie

18' x 11' 8" (5.49 x 3.56 m)

Spain

IT DOES NOT OFTEN HAPPEN that a carpet from one country is confused with one from another. Styles, design, and traditions are usually readily associated with particular nations.

But there are exceptions, as in the case of this carpet from Spain. Certain characteristics, such as use of color, remind one of the French Aubusson genre. Closer analysis, however, points to one specific difference: the lack of restraint.

In an Aubusson carpet, the design would have been more "open" and with much less intricate detail. This Spanish carpet, on the other hand, expresses exuberant detail—from arabesques to flower-filled urns, with formality and simplicity interwoven with classical attributes. This is hardly surprising, given the great difference in temperaments between the French and the Spanish, not to mention the distinctive traditions of each country.

This very special carpet pays passing homage to the Aubusson genre, then goes on to reveal its particularly Iberian roots.

PLATE 89

The steel-blue field has ivory-colored cartouches containing vases, around a large, central, molded cartouche, with radiating floral sprays and central flowerhead. It is contained within a fox-brown frame, in a light blue roundel border with ivory-colored floral lozenges.

Late 19th-Century Savonnerie

18' x 11' (5.49 x 3.35 m)

France

SAVONNERIE CARPETS are usually known for their gentility. A Savonnerie carpet expresses a way of life devoid entirely of struggle and commerce. A gentleness and contemplativeness are reflected in their beauty.

In this larger-than-average carpet, we find all the hallmarks of a truly fine Savonnerie—soft colors, gentle flowers, ribbons, and wreaths.

PLATE 90

The shaded ivory-colored field has acanthus and floral sprays around a large floral roundel, contained within a shaded ivory-colored floral frame, in a striped border.

LATE 19TH-CENTURY SAVONNERIE

14' 4" x 8' 5" (4.37 x 2.57 m)

FRANCE

THE COLORS OF NATURE are never lacking in harmony. The same cannot always be said for human artworks, though. In fact, an awkward juxtaposition of certain colors is often deliberate—a kind of shattering of recognized harmony and form to underline a specific intention.

Certain artists make a point of this, but it is almost unknown in the realm of classical carpets, perhaps because weavers reflect a preoccupation with Nature's harmony in their carpets. The classical form, in spite of many magnificent interpretative variations, demands that the weaver adhere strictly to time-honored formulae.

In this Savonnerie, for example, one can see a controlled design offset by imaginative *joie de vivre*. It is a fiery interpretation of a well-known format. The most notable features are obviously the freeform swags embellishing the center circle with its bouquet of flowers. On first impression, the design seems to be somewhat extravagant, but later reveals itself to be precise and very deliberate. The overall effect is one of exuberance set within a border so formal that any inclination to frivolity is held in perfect restraint.

PLATE 91

The dusty rose field has golden, green, aubergine-, and rose-colored acanthus sprays around a large ivory-colored floral medallion with similar rounded pendants. It is contained within a blue border of oak leaves and ribbons with stylized floral cartouches, between plain stripes.

Early 19th-Century Aubusson

15' 2" x 12' 9" (4.62 x 3.89 m)

France

———— ⋄ ————

NO OTHER CARPET MAKERS in the western hemisphere have ever produced floral masterpieces to equal this magnificent Aubusson. Even on the closest inspection, every petal on every flower stands out in perfectly.

Few painters ever achieve such dimensional accuracy. It says a lot about the excellence of design associated with the Aubusson studios, and even more about the master weavers who carried out the work—for here one sees the ultimate tribute both to carpet design and quality of manufacture.

The centerpiece succeeds in obeying the strictest rule of good design: to lead the eye to the focal point of the whole work. Like some fabulous jewel, every facet of the centerpiece is clearly defined and in high relief. Every color variation blends perfectly with the rest of the carpet. This carpet is indeed a masterpiece.

Plate 92

The apricot-hued field has shaded rust-red and dark brown, stylized, floral, cruciform, lozenge medallions around a central, dark brown, floral, radiating medallion. It is contained within a dark brown floral border, between plain stripes.

EARLY 20TH-CENTURY AUBUSSON

15' x 14' 4" (4.57 x 4.37 m)

FRANCE

PATHWAYS AND CENTERPIECES that suggest grand formal gardens have always been a source of inspiration for creators of fine carpets. Even geometric influences often give way to (or combine with) floral tributes.

Such interdependence illustrates the influence of Nature upon art—perhaps even vice-versa.

However we view the matter, great carpets such as this wonderful Aubusson often reflect Nature, and being woven from pure wool and colored with vegetable dyes, complete the basic dependence of the one on the other.

One notes many echoes of classical garden layout in this fine Aubusson, and it is easy to imagine that such a garden did, in fact, influence the carpet design. Perhaps even the famous garden at the Palace of Versailles might have served as inspiration for the carpet makers.

PLATE 93

The shaded rust-colored field has apricot-hued tracery flowerheads around a large brown, ivory-colored, and golden floral garland border, in an ivory-colored cusped and stylized floral frame. It is contained within a dark brown border of floral vines, with outer plain stripe.

Late 19th-Century Aubusson

11' 8" x 8' (3.56 x 2.44 m)

France

———— ◈ ————

Compared with most Aubusson carpets, this comparatively small piece is deliberately pale and limpid.

It belongs in that special location where the decor is muted and elegant—a boudoir, perhaps, or a second drawing room where fine furniture and beautiful portraits harmonize softly.

Such an environment would reflect a very feminine ambiance: a harpsichord in the corner, for example, and echo a bygone era of elegance, which has been hopelessly lost in the tangle of the 20th century.

Such places must still exist—hidden away discreetly in the houses of a few discerning patrons.

Plate 94

The pale champagne field has a central pale bouquet surrounded by floral swags forming a medallion, contained within a scrolling floral frame with vases and acanthus, in a plain minor striped border.

EARLY 19TH-CENTURY AUBUSSON

9' x 7' (2.74 x 2.13 m)

FRANCE

HERE WE HAVE AN ALMOST PERFECT REPLICA of the famous Baccarat paperweight, known as a "Millifiori," leading one to suppose that the popular 19th-century paperweight design influenced this Aubusson carpet.

The repetitive motif is very eyecatching, and the rigidity of the design is very hypnotic. Is it a field of flowers? A garden within a cascading border of entwining creepers? Or simply a floral tribute to a handsome room?

PLATE 95

The apricot-colored field has columns of ivory-, shaded aubergine-, and tomato-colored, stellar floral roundels surrounded by entwined, plain golden vines. It is contained within a broad ivory-and-apricot-colored border, divided by an elaborately flowering vine.

Mid-19th-Century Needlework

10' 9" x 8' (3.28 x 2.44 m)

France

—◆—

THERE IS A FINE LINE between what is merely excellent craftsmanship and what is truly a work of art. Sometimes, it is hard to distinguish between the two.

Tapestry making is an art form that has been practiced for centuries around the world, and has been long associated with Europe.

France, of course, is particularly renowned for her tapestries. In earlier times, ladies of leisure—of wealth and station—acquired the techniques purely as a means of idling away the hours.

Here one sees a commercial tapestry, typical of the late 19th century in France. Few tapestries, however, reveal such innate artistry. The pattern is intricate and technically involved and demanded precise manipulation of needles and wools. The workmanship is so precise, in fact, that one can certainly say that here a work of craftsmanship has crossed the line and become a work of art.

PLATE 96

The ivory-colored field has four columns of steel-gray scalloped medallions with rose-colored cruciform centerpieces and hooked blood-red tendrils. It is contained within a wine-colored border of acanthus and tendrils with inner floral stripe.

Late 19th-Century Needlework

8' x 6' 3" (2.44 x 1.91 m)

France

IN THIS NEEDLEWORK PANEL from France, one is confronted with a large number of elements to appreciate: its obvious eye appeal, attractive use of colors, its lovely design, and its metaphorical associations. Is the panel intended to have an architectural feeling, for example, or is it merely a clever juxtaposition of angles and cartouche?

Whatever one's reaction to this piece, no one can deny its tremendous eye appeal. Does its "busy-ness" contribute to its special charm or detract from it? Are the definitions exact enough or are they so intricate that time must be spent examining their interactions?

This is not a readily understood piece, but one thing is very apparent: it exhibits great mastery and creativity. It begs to be noticed and rewards closer inspection.

PLATE 97

The dark brown field has three columns of tan cusped and stepped panels, containing bouquets divided by stylized, floral cruciform motifs in a broad reciprocal frame of stylized, cusped floral motifs. It is contained within a similar minor motif border, with outer stylized egg and dark stripe.

Early 19th-Century Tapestry

9' 4" x 8' 3" (2.84 x 2.51 m)

France

FOUR GRANDEES HUNTING IN THE FOREST seem no match for the fearless bird sitting on a pole; yet, it appears indifferent to the enormous arrow pointed—not too accurately—in its direction.

Be that as it may, no self-respecting bird could fail to be impressed by the attire of such would-be executioners—especially when immortality was guaranteed by inclusion in such a magnificent French tapestry!

Here, we see attention to detail reminiscent of tapestries of a much earlier period, when artistic standards were extremely high.

The magnificent framework-border need hardly be pointed out—the luxurious combination of fruit and foliage is simply glorious.

Few works of art can be ascribed as accurately as this French tapestry. By the time it was created, France could rightfully claim dominance in the field. This splendid example offers ample illustration of why.

Plate 98

Elaborately customed figures are standing in a clearing in a wood, one aiming a bow at a perching bird target, surrounded by a wide variety of trees, plants in the foreground, a town in the background. It is contained within a broad border of acanthus and scrolling vines, with perching birds and pomegranates and a variety of other fruit, between plain stripes.

Early 18th-Century Tapestry

7' 8" x 7' 4" (2.34 x 2.24 m)

France

―――― ·◇· ――――

TAPESTRIES OFFER US MANY REASONS why imagination is the key to human creativity and frequently leads to remarkable works of art.

In this tapestry, for example, we see a strictly controlled use of such imaginative symbols as winged angels alongside a fantasy scene of what appears to be St. George slaying the Dragon and rescuing the damsel in distress.

It is clear that no constraints were placed on the artisans, with the result that artistic license is perfectly balanced with the use of color and classical inspiration—the true formula for a great work of art.

Plate 99

The mythological figures are witnessing Saint George about to slay the Dragon, set in a wooded landscape with sea beyond, contained within a plain blue border.